A NET OF FIREFLIES

蚊帳の中に螢放ちてアヽ楽しや

蕪村

STARRY NIGHT *by Tomoda Sôgyo,* re-creating a haiku by Buson:
*What a delightful game it is to set
Fireflies loose in bed beneath the net!*

A NET OF FIREFLIES

JAPANESE HAIKU AND HAIKU PAINTINGS

with verse translations
and an essay
by
HAROLD STEWART

CHARLES E. TUTTLE COMPANY : PUBLISHERS
Rutland, Vermont   *Tokyo, Japan*

European Representatives

For the Continent:
BOXERBOOKS, INC., *Zurich*

For the British Isles:
MARK PATERSON & CO. LTD., *London*

Published by
Charles E. Tuttle Company
of Rutland, Vermont & Tokyo, Japan
with editorial offices at
15 Edogawa-cho, Bunkyo-ku, Tokyo

© *1960 by Charles E. Tuttle Co.*
All Rights Reserved

Library of Congress
Catalog Card No. 60-15603

First edition, 1960
Second printing, 1961

Book design & typography
by M. Weatherby

MANUFACTURED IN JAPAN

TABLE OF CONTENTS

mada Junji, with thanks to those artists who live and in memory of those departed. On behalf of all these genial haijin, the publishers and I welcome the opportunity of providing these examples of this little-known aspect of Japanese art.

Whatever accuracy there may be in the following verses is due to my predecessors in translation; while any poetic merit they may possess is the inspiration of Benten, the Japanese Goddess of Music and Poetry.

HAROLD STEWART

Melbourne, August, 1960

ACKNOWLEDGMENTS

I would like to express my gratitude to Mr. Geoffrey Fairbairn of Melbourne and Mr. Harvey Mason of Sydney, whose unexpected and spontaneous generosity helped materially with this work. I am also indebted to Mr. Leslie Oates for valuable technical suggestions, to Mr. Peter Kelly for editorial assistance, to Mr. Gordon Kirby for arranging publication in Japan, and to Mr. Meredith Weatherby for designing the book and discovering the illustrations.

Special thanks are due to the respective publishers for permission to make quotations from the works of Alan Watts, D. T. Suzuki, R. H. Blyth, A. Miyamori, H. G. Henderson, and Arthur Waley. These quotations appear in the essay at the end of this volume.

The frontispiece was specially painted for this book by the well-known Japanese artist Tomoda Toshio, whose "haiku" name is Sôgyo. All the other illustrations have been selected from the four volumes of the *Gendai Haiga Shû* (Collection of Modern Haiga), edited and published by Shimada Yûkichi under the imprint of his publishing house, the Haigadô (Haiga Pavilion), Tokyo, 1915–17. This publication contained some 119 haiku paintings (*haiga* in Japanese), by 37 of Japan's leading contemporary haijin, skilfully reproduced in color by wood blocks. It was a limited edition which has long been out of print, the Haigadô is no longer in existence, and only a few of the artists are known to be still living. The paintings are reproduced here by kind permission of the publisher's grandson, Shi-

LIST OF ILLUSTRATIONS

SPRING

"*Le secret d'ennuyer est celui de tout dire.*"
—VOLTAIRE

THE GESTURE

"Be careful not to break my flowering tree!"
He warned; and broke a branch of plum for me.
                                        —TAIGI

ONE SENSE OF BEAUTY

On white plum-petals that were pure and sweet,
The nightingale now wipes its muddy feet.
                                        —ISSA

MORE THAN FORGIVEN

Plum-blossoms give their fragrance still to him
Whose thoughtless hand has broken off their limb.
                                        —CHIYO

AFTER THE FISHING-BOATS DEPART

The tall white sails emerge above the bay's
Low and level veils of morning haze.
                                        —GAKOKU

THE SPRING SEA

All day, with gently undulating swell,
The spring sea rose and fell, and rose and fell. . . .
                                        —BUSON

THE RECLUSE

In my ten-foot bamboo hut this spring,
There is nothing: there is everything.
                    —SODÔ

REBIRTH

Ah, for the heart whose winter knew no doubt,
The white plum-blossoms, first to venture out!
                    —MOKUIN

THE ENTRANCE OF SPRING

The scene is almost set for spring to come:
A hazy moon and blossoms on the plum. . . .
                    —BASHÔ

UNCONVENTIONAL DEBUT

The little nightingale of buff and brown
Singing its first spring quaver—upside down!
                    —KIKAKU

ON THE ROAD TO NARA

Because of early spring, this nameless hill
Is knee-deep in the gauze of morning still.
                    —BASHÔ

SHOOTS OF THE HORSETAIL PLANT *by Saitô Shôshû*

PLUM–BLOSSOMS THROUGH A HERMITAGE WINDOW *by Nakamura Fusetsu*

SPRING CALM

The Inland Sea at twilight: star by star,
The lamps shine out on islands, near and far. . . .
—SHIKI

A MUSICAL EVENING

The geisha's pose is shadowed on the screen
Beside a willow sapling, fledged with green.
—HÔ-ô

UNFATHOMED

Without a sound, the white camellia fell
To sound the darkness of the deep stone well.
—BUSON

SPRING DAWN

Up comes the bucket from the well of gloom,
And in it floats—a pink camellia bloom.
—KAKEI

SUDDEN SPRING

With tender impact on the icy air,
The peach-buds burst: their silken petals flare.
—HÔ-ô

CORRESPONDENCE

Among the peach-tree blossoms—ah, the glow
Of sunrise wakes a cock with scarlet crow!
                                        —KIKAKU

THE MASTER STROKE

A seedling shoulders up some crumbs of ground:
The fields are suddenly green for miles around!
                                        —HÔ-Ô

FIRST PUDDLE

Though spring rain patters on the mud, as yet
The froglets' sallow bellies are not wet.
                                        —BUSON

A SHELTER OF LEAVES

A sparrow, springing on this bamboo-cane,
Chirps at the downward sound of steady rain.
                                        —HÔ-Ô

GARDEN AFTER RAIN

Why, as that single tea-camellia fell,
It spilled bright water from its heavy bell!
                                        —BASHÔ

MOUNTAIN TEMPLE IN SPRING *by Suzuki Koson*

DEMON AND VIOLETS *by Nishi Ōshû*

VIEWPOINT

I climb the pagoda, five storeys high:
There, on that fir-top, sits a butterfly!
—KASO

FROM A HILLSIDE

The rice-fields spread their flooded terracing
Of mirrors: segments in a beetle's wing.
—HÔ-Ô

SPRING SNOWFLAKE

A white-queued egret, balanced on the breeze,
Sails through the dark-green cryptomeria trees.
—RAIZAN

AT NARA

There sat the great bronze Buddha. From his hollow
Nostril suddenly darted out—a swallow!
—ISSA

BOUNDLESS COMPASSION

Oh, weak and skinny frog, though death is near,
Fight on and don't give in: Issa is here!
—ISSA

THE SILENT REBUKE

Angrily I returned; awaiting me
Within my court—the tranquil willow-tree.
                                    —RYÔTA

A FLOWERING BIRD

The pheasant's eyes are gold, but ringed with red:
Two tea-camellias flowering in his head.
                                    —HÔ-Ô

IN A TEMPLE GARDEN

The old green pond is silent; here the hop
Of a frog plumbs the evening stillness: plop![1]
                                    —BASHÔ

THE LIKENESS OF WIND

The flurried willow paints the breeze's rush
Without the need for paper, ink, or brush.
                                    —SARYÛ

THE EXECUTIONERS

A red camellia drops to the garden bed,
Where scurrying rats drag off its severed head.
                                    —SHICHIKU

SENSITIVE

The butterfly, lifted on the spring wind's billow,
Alights elsewhere upon the swaying willow.

—BASHÔ

ONE NOTE OF ZEN

A frog had plucked his slack-stringed samisen:
The pond was quieter at nightfall, then.

—HÔ-Ô

DISCOVERY

Again the cherry-buds are bursting through:
Horses have four legs! Birds have only two!

—ONITSURA

WONDER

I saw afar a vast white cloud—but no!
That was Yoshino's mount of flowering snow.

—TEISHITSU

THE DEVOTEE

My shanks grow thin? As long as they can climb,
Expect me, Yoshino, in blossom time.

—BASHÔ

THE POET

I came to praise the cherry-blossom: "Oh! . . .
Oh! . . ." That's all, upon Mount Yoshino.
—TEISHITSU

THE DAIMYO

The noble lord gets off his horse. And who
Makes him dismount? The cherry-blossoms do.
—ISSA

THE SAMURAI

No friends today— Oh, let me meet no friends
Until my leave for blossom-viewing ends!
—KYORAI

GOING HOME

White cherry-blossoms in the sunset blaze:
I stand, my breast against my staff, and gaze. . . .
—SÔ-A

SLIGHT INTERRUPTION

Ah, nightingale, with half your song expressed,
I leave for the next world—to hear the rest!
—AN ANONYMOUS PRISONER
CONDEMNED TO DEATH

FROM MY WINDOW AT TWILIGHT

A cloud of flowers. A booming temple-bell.
Ueno's or Asakusa's? Who can tell?
—BASHÔ

ATMOSPHERE

How still it is! The belfry's vibrant boom
Does not so much as stir the cherry-bloom.
—FUHAKU

AT THE FERRY

Through the spring rain a ferryboat is oared,
Paper umbrellas, high and low, aboard.
—SHIKI

THE EIGHT FAMOUS VIEWS OF ÔMI

Mist hid the other seven views. Ah well,
I heard the Mii Temple's evening bell![2]
—BASHÔ

ON A JOURNEY

Wearied, and seeking shelter for the night—
Ah, these wistaria flowers refresh the sight!
—BASHÔ

LETTER AND SPIRIT

My ears had found the sermon dull and stale;
But in the woods outside—the nightingale!
—SHIKI

ON THE DEATH OF HIS CHILD

His life: a dream in spring, as brief, as sad. . . .
Oh, pity me that I have not gone mad!
—RAIZAN

A STREET IN EDO

Through this shower in spring, at dusk dispersing,
A raincoat and umbrella stroll, conversing. . . .
—BUSON

BEFORE NIGHTFALL

With willows drooping overhead, they light
The lamps upon the palace gates tonight.
—SHIKI

THE SPRING FESTIVAL

What pains I took to hang my lantern on
The branch of cherry-blossom, where it shone!
—SHIKI

猫に恋ある
淋しくひ芽を女

WALKING ALONE IN SPRING *by Okano Sakae*

TADPOLES IN SPRING WATERS *by Kosugi Misei*

ROMANCE

Evening in spring: the fox's phantom played
A young and gallant prince in masquerade.[3]
—BUSON

BY STARLIGHT

How the racemes of white wistaria sway,
As though the night wind blew the Milky Way!
—HAJIN

THE CATCH

I shook my net where whitebait seemed to thresh:
A shoal of moonbeams slithered through the mesh.
—ÔTÔ

EXCAVATIONS BY NIGHT

At dawn my violets grew aslant: a hole
Was tunnelled underneath them by a mole.
—BONCHÔ

ON A HIGH PASS

Above the mountain's snow-white vapour floats
An airy voice: the skylark's rising notes.
—KYOROKU

NATURALLY

How heart-appealing, on the mountain-pass,
Are wild violets hidden in the grass!
—BASHÔ

AT NISHIGÔ RAPIDS

Has the cascade shaken with rushing sound
These yellow kerria petals toward the ground?
—BASHÔ

TRANSPARENT PRESENCE

A veering school of lancelets was inferred
Only because the water's clearness stirred.
—RAIZAN

VIEW OF KÔRIYAMA

With roof on roof, the white stone castle towers
Above a plain of golden mustard-flowers.
—KYOROKU

RETURN OF THE DISPOSSESSED

The same old village: here where I was born,
Every flower I touch—a hidden thorn.
—ISSA

THE ORPHANS

Oh, ragged sparrow without any mother,
When we are lonely, let's play with each other!
                              —ISSA (aged 6)

SUNSHOWER

Warm sunshine through a clearing after showers;
And for a while, the scent of hawthorn flowers.
                              —KYOSHI

STILL UNION

Single butterflies dancing through the air
Until they meet: how motionless a pair!
                              —BASHÔ

BONDAGE

The caged bird gazes at the butterflies
Beyond the bars with longing—watch its eyes!
                              —ISSA

LIBERATION

The skylark's song above the meadow-flowers
Would last for longer than the day has hours.
                              —BASHÔ

IN THE MEADOW

Oh who, untouched by tenderness, can pass
Small white daisies scattered in the grass?
—HÔ-Ô

FAIR WARNING

Young sparrows, ruffled in a dust-bath, fly
Out of the way! My horse is plodding by.
—ISSA

UNDERCURRENT

A cumbersome waggon rumbled down the hill
Under its load: my peonies tremble still.
—BUSON

SOWN WITH GOLD

How far these fields of flowering mustard run:
East to the moonrise, west to the setting sun!
—BUSON

TRANSMIGRATION

Lighting one candle with another's flame
At dusk in spring—the same, yet not the same.
—BUSON

LISTENING TO THE SKYLARK *by Shibahara Kaizô*

FALLING PETALS AND PARASOL *by Kikakudô Kiichi*

EPITOME OF SPRING

Glimpsed through a crevice in the garden fence,
One white flower is spring's impermanence.
—BUSON

AND SO

And so the spring buds burst, and so I gaze,
And so the blossoms fall, and so my days. . . .
—ONITSURA

BURNT OUT

Onto the ashes where my cottage burned,
The cherry-blossoms scatter, unconcerned.
—HOKUSHI

ONE SPRING DAY

How fragile, how ephemeral in flight
This life—for instance: butterfly, alight!
—SÔIN

DOWN THE AVENUE

The curtain of the daimyo's palanquin
Was lifted. Cherry-petals drifted in.
—MÔGAN

THE DELICATE TOUCH

Violets in retirement near its trail
Are touched in passing by the pheasant's tail.
                    —SHŪSHIKI

RAPE OF SPRING

The cherry-petals' loosely fluttering swarm
Is put to flight; in dark pursuit—the storm!
                    —SADAIE

THE MIDDLE WAY

A white swan swimming to the shore beyond
Parts with his breast the cherry-petalled pond.
                    —RÔKA

ILLUSION

The fallen blossoms which I saw arise,
Returning toward the bough, were butterflies.
                    —MORITAKE

A RAIN-SPOILT SPRING

The end of spring has turned the scattered bloom
To torn waste paper for the bamboo broom.
                    —BUSON

SUMMER

WAKING AT AN INN

Through white mosquito-nets, as yet undrawn,
How cool the bay looks in the summer dawn!
—SÔSEKI

THE PAVILION ON THE LAKE

Here in the morning cool, the breezes waft
The perfume from the lotus-blooms aloft.
—RIMPÛ

UNSEEN TILL NOW

How visibly the gentle morning airs
Stir in the caterpillar's silky hairs!
—BUSON

REFRESHING

So cool the summer melons look, a few
Spattered with mud-flecks from the morning dew.
—BASHÔ

COUNTRY REFINEMENT

The stooping women plant their rice along
The terrace—soiled in everything but song.
—RAIZAN

WITH SHARPENED SENSES

When tall green blades have pierced the iris bed,
The cuckoo's pointed cry strikes overhead.

—BASHÔ

INNOCENCE

The newborn foal, who stands with knock-kneed pose,
Over the iris flowers pokes out his nose.

—ISSA

SOUND OF THE CROSS

The cuckoo's singing as it speeds along
Inscribes a cross against the skylark's song.

—KYORAI

SUMMER WATERCOLOUR

The iris standing in the marsh: so blue,
Its roots have drunk the sky's reflected hue.

—HÔ-Ô

RICH APPAREL

The happy beggar, whom the passer loathes,
Wears Earth and Heaven as his summer clothes.

—KIKAKU

HIGH CLOUDS AT NOON *by Ogawa Senô*

RIVER BREEZE *by Ishikawa Kinichirô*

THE NOON CONVOLVULUS

Ah! It will never wash its face of blue
In dew of morning or in evening dew.[4]
—YAYU

BROWSING

This butterfly which on a poppy clings
Opens and shuts a booklet's paper wings.
—HÔ-Ô

PURE QUALITY

Lilies that lean across my brushwood fence:
Have clouds of snow a whiteness so intense?
—SHIKÔ

PRELUDE FOR KOTO

A lightning-flash! The liquid chime of dew
Dripping throughout the forest-high bamboo.
—BUSON

INVENTION

People caught by suddenly pouring skies:
What ingenious hats they improvise!
—OTSUYÛ

HIROSHIGE'S "RAINSTORM AT SUWARA"

Against the slant grey rain, in silhouette,
Men and mules are hurrying through the wet.

—HÔ-Ô

THE MONSOON

"How humid are the rains!" I said; whereat
A large ant walked across my rice-straw mat.

—SHIRÔ

SAMIDARE

The downpour prickles on the pond, so sharp
It hits the heads of shallow-floating carp.

—SHIKI

THE WATERFALL

Its threads of water widen with the rain
Day after day, until they twist a skein.

—FUHAKU

DISCORDANT QUARTET

Four magpies on a crooked pine-tree fork;
Their harsh beaks gape, and quarrelsome their talk.

—HÔ-Ô

THE GARDEN OF RYÔAN-JI

Mossbound and weatherworn, the boulders stand;
Around them flows a stream of silver sand.[5]

—HÔ-Ô

THE ARTIST

His brush abruptly leaps and flicks and swishes:
Swiftly across the paper swim three fishes.

—HÔ-Ô

THE TASTE OF TEA

Whisked to a boiling emerald froth, the cha
Is passed around. We sip its flavour: Ah!

—HÔ-Ô

DANCERS OF OLD KYOTO

The geisha flirt their fans; their sashes trail;
Like goldfish undulating fins and tail.

—GETTO

DEEP REFLECTION

Patiently fishing in the lake, the crane's
Long red legs have shortened since the rains.

—BASHÔ

THE ART OF ARCHERY

After the sudden shower, along the strand
Green pine-needles are sticking in the sand.

—SHIKI

THE OPPOSITES

With flowering tongues, the honeysuckle twines
Among the aloe's armament of spines.

—HÔ-Ô

FRIGHTENED DELIGHT

A sudden downpour! Thunderclouds are cracking!
And round the farmhouse all the ducks run, quacking!

—KIKAKU

HOME-GROWN

Washed by monsoonal summer's rainy weeks,
How chill and white, how fresh and green, are leeks!

—BASHÔ

ANOTHER DAY, ANOTHER WAY

Between the barley's bending ears of grain,
The path has narrowed since the heavy rain.

—JÔSÔ

BATH IN SUMMER *by Ōta Saburô*

SONG OF A SUMMER SHOWER *by Yûki Somei*

KOAN

What if a housefly on the swatter stands
In perfect faith, and wipes its feet and hands?
—ZEN PARADOX

KANNON'S ANSWER

Oh, do not kill that fly! It would entreat:
See how it wrings its little hands and feet!
—ISSA

MIDSUMMER VIGIL

Dawn already, after the shortest night,
Has dimmed the harbour lanterns, still alight.
—SHIKI

LIVING IN POVERTY

Though faint and from afar, the cool breeze comes
Crookedly down my alley in the slums.
—ISSA

RICH REMINISCENCE

Those noonday naps: the paper hut so small,
My feet pressed gingerly against the wall.
—BASHÔ

BEDMATES

Dreaming of battles, was I slain in fight?
I'm peppered with rosettes: those fleas can bite!
—KIKAKU

AN APOLOGY

Sorry my hut's so small; but you are free
To do your jumping practice, Mr. Flea.
—ISSA

SUMMER AT NIKKÔ

A glittering sea of green and gold, they shine,
The sunlit leaves submerging Nikkô Shrine.
—BASHÔ

STARTLED

Out of the golden hall the swallow's fright
Escapes with swift calligraphy of flight.
—BUSON

IN THE FOREST

The fawn with sunbeam-spotted coat in vain
Shakes off the butterfly, to doze again.
—ISSA

INTOXICATION

A furry bee nuzzles amid the head
Of yellow ginger-blossoms pronged with red.

              —HÔ-Ô

"BUT THOSE UNHEARD . . ."

Deep in the summer shade, when leaves were mute,
I heard the Suma Temple's unblown flute.

              —BASHÔ

WANDERER FROM THE WORLD

Deepen, O cuckoo in the wood, my mood
Of mutability, my solitude. . . .

              —BASHÔ

WEATHERWISE

Midsummer must have come: the carp all doze,
Each supping air with half-protruded nose.

              —RAIZAN

HEAD-HIGH, THE PAMPAS GRASS

Crossing the summer moor, what guides our course?
The hay a peasant shoulders for his horse.

              —BASHÔ

FEAR

The snake has slid away; but still its eyes
Glare at me from the grass and paralyse.

—KYOSHI

THE RUINS OF TAKADACHI FORT

Over the warriors summer grasses wave:
The aftermath of dreams, however brave.

—BASHÔ

SPLIT BY THE WIND

The butterfly, with airy stitches, sews
Together again the barley's parted rows.

—SORA

SILENCE

A frail white butterfly, beneath the spell
Of noon, is sleeping on the huge bronze bell.

—BUSON

MIDSUMMER LULL

How hot, on afternoons without a breeze,
The cobwebs hanging from the dusty trees!

—ONITSURA

SUDDEN DOWNPOUR *by Shibahara Kaizô*

SHY RAINBOW *by Hirafuku Hyakusui*

A RAUCOUS SOLITUDE

What burning stillness! Brass cicada-drones
Drill their resonance into rocks and stones.
—BASHÔ

THE TORTOISE-SHELL CAT

The brazen sunflower glowed, as underneath
A tigress bore her cub between her teeth.
—BUSHI

AFTER THE DEATH OF HER SMALL SON

Alas! How far beyond recall today,
My hunter after dragonflies, you stray!
—CHIYO

WITH MINDLESS SKILL

The erratic swallow, as it dips and veers,
Almost grazes the nodding barley-ears.
—IZAN

IRONICAL

How hot the pedlar, panting with his pack
Of fans—a load of breezes on his back!
—KAKÔ

PRIMEVAL BREATH

High in the air the mounting cloud-mass swells,
Over the dried marsh where a python dwells.
                                    —SHIKI

ETERNAL LIFE

A shrill cicada dinning: from its cry,
None could foretell how quickly it must die.[6]
                                    —BASHÔ

SATORI

I bowed before the Buddha, now obscure,
Now bright with lightning, on the stormy moor.
                                    —KAKEI

INDRA'S NET

The sun-shower, mirrored in a globe of rain,
Hangs for one moment, never seen again.
                                    —HÔ-Ô

LATE VICTORY

The thunderstorm retreating, sunset still
Burns on a tree in which cicadas shrill.
                                    —SHIKI

THE RIVER'S MOUTH

Swollen by floods, Mogami's estuary
Swallowed the red-hot sunball undersea.
—BASHÔ

HIDDEN INFLUENCE

A Buddhist sutra, calmly chanted, fills
With cool refreshing air the fields and hills.
—KYORAI

DEATH BY ECSTASY

Discarded, one cicada's casket lay:
Did it utterly sing itself away?
—BASHÔ

RELAXATION

The evening cool: enjoyed beneath the sallows,
Paddling amid my shadow in the shallows.
—BUSON

ISSA'S ADVICE

You plump green watermelons, keeping cool,
Turn into frogs, if boys pass by your pool!
—ISSA

RUSTIC SECURITY

I shut my brushwood gate; but should that fail
To stop intruders, for a lock—this snail!

—ISSA

A SLICE OF MELON

The melon-fields lie waiting under skies
Of sultry darkness for the moon to rise.

—SORA

THE METEOR

Just as that firefly, glowing on a spray
Of leaves, dropped off—it suddenly shot away!

—BASHÔ

FIRST GLIMPSE

Monsoonal rains; and then one night there shines,
As though by stealth, the moon between the pines.

—RYÔTA

SITTING ON KYORAI'S VERANDA

A cuckoo called! The moonlight filters through
Shadow-shifting thickets of cool bamboo.

—BASHÔ

CHORUS OF CICADAS AFTER RAIN *by Okano Sakae*

PUMPKIN HARVEST *by Sasaki Rimpû*

AFTER THE HEAT

A moonlit evening: here beside the pool,
Stripped to the waist, a snail enjoys the cool.

—ISSA

ON A DRAWING BY SOKEI-AN

The black cat's face: an unexpected dawn
Has swallowed midnight in a wide pink yawn.

—HÔ-Ô

FLORAL REPAIRS

The morning-glory flowers have opened, patching
My hermitage's roof, which needed thatching.

—ISSA

THE TASK

O timid snail, by nature weak and lowly,
Crawl up the cone of Fuji slowly, slowly. . . .

—ISSA

RESIDUES

A snail has left its netted trail: the faint
And silver sutra written by a saint.

—HÔ-Ô

BEING AND BECOMING

The sun set on the swamp with orange glare;
A ball of gnats revolving in the air.

—HÔ-Ô

BY THE MERE

An evening breeze across the reedy banks:
Ripples around the blue-grey heron's shanks.

—BUSON

THE OLD FOLLY

The octopus, while summer moonshine streams
Into the trap, enjoys its fleeting dreams.

—BASHÔ

STILL AND CLEAR

A sea beach silvered by the moon; and then
Nearby, the cries of distant fishermen.

—SHÛRIN

NEHAN

A cuckoo's cry is lost in silence, while
Vanishing toward a solitary isle. . . .[7]

—BASHÔ

AUTUMN

THE GATELESS GATE

Through morning mists and murmurs from the sea
Emerges—one vermilion torii.

—KIKAKU

UNREGARDED DIADEM

Dew on the brambles delicately worn
At sunrise: one clear drop on every thorn.

—BUSON

AT THE WELL

Around the bucket, morning-glories cling:
I beg for water at another spring.

—CHIYO

WITH EVERY BREEZE

The lespedeza blossoms dip and sway,
Yet never spill the dewdrops from their spray.[8]

—BASHÔ

STRANGERS

How soon the morning-glory's hour must end!
Alas! It, too, can never be my friend. . . .

—BASHÔ

ALIVE

So much vitality in so few inches:
A perch of hopping, chirping, spotted finches!
—HÔ-Ô

NO RESPITE

Feast of the Dead: but even on this day,
Smoke from the burning-ground is blown away.
—BASHÔ

CLINGING

This world is but a single dewdrop, set
Trembling upon a stem; and yet . . . and yet . . .[9]
—ISSA

THE MEANING OF LIFE

A yearly sweep for our parental tomb:
The youngest child comes carrying the broom.
—ISSA

THE MEANING OF DEATH

Going to tend our family graves today,
The old dog trots ahead to show the way.
—ISSA

AUTUMN IN A MOUNTAIN VILLAGE *by Ishikawa Kinichirô*

BIRD SNARE *by Kosugi Misei*

THE DIAMOND SPHERE

Let all my life of dust be cleansed in you,
O one clear evanescent drop of dew!
—BASHÔ

A DYING HOUSE

The household standing by the ancestral graves
Are all white-haired, and lean upon their staves.
—BASHÔ

ON THE NIGHT OF THE DEPARTED

Returning through the cedar-pillared park
Are festive lanterns—fireflies in the dark.[10]
—HÔ-Ô

GONE OUT

The paper lanterns on the graves are torn
By heavy dew in the chill autumn dawn.
—RANKÔ

"INTO THE SHINING SEA"

The sunlit dews dry up and disappear;
This world defiles: they would not linger here.
—ISSA

WITHOUT WORDS

What message would the wild bush-clover utter,
Gently brushing, brushing against my shutter?
—SESSHI

THE LIGHT OF TRANQUILITY

The frenzied dash and dart of dragonflies
Is stilled: a crescent moon begins to rise.
—KIKAKU

A MONTH AGO

The new moon showed its silver rim of light;
I watched and waited since, and lo: tonight![11]
—BASHÔ

THE GIFT OF EMPTINESS

Retiring into the shadows, I bestow
My guest-room on the moon's approaching glow.
—SEIBI

TREASURE

The moon—how big and round and red and bright!
Children, to whom does it belong tonight?
—ISSA

MOST PRECIOUS POSSESSION

Still on my window-sill the moon is left:
The thief has overlooked it in his theft.
—RYÔKAN

A RACE OF POETS

Full moon tonight: and is there in the land
A Japanese without a brush in hand?
—ONITSURA

TRIAL AND ERROR

I hung the bright moon on a pine-branch there;
Then took it off, and hung it on elsewhere.
—HOKUSHI

THE HUMAN FORM

Moonlight has sketched the shadow from a pine:
How elegant its pose, compared with mine!
—BAISHITSU

THE CRAFTSMAN

O moon in autumn, could some artisan
Carve you a handle—what a perfect fan!
—SÔKAN

UNDER THE SAME ROOF

Courtesans at the inn and I commune:
Wild hagi blossoms and the spotless moon.
— BASHÔ

SQUARE, TRIANGLE, AND CIRCLE

Beneath the bed's mosquito-net, I tie
One corner up: the harvest moon is high.
—CHIYO

AFTER THE DEATH OF HER LOVER

Sitting or lying, still I wake. How wide
The net is now, with no one at my side!
—UKIHASHI

AUTUMN VIGIL

The guests had gone; but till the full moon set,
I watched in bed with no mosquito-net.
—RYÔTA

LAST SIGNATURE

The moon has shown its selfless light to me;
As for this world,
        I am,
            respectfully,
—CHIYO

PAMPAS GRASS *by Kikakudô Kiichi*

HUNTER AND DEER *by Nishi Ōshū*

THE MIRRORS OF BUDDHAHOOD

These worlds of dew, minute, translucent, bright,
Do not discriminate where they alight.

—SÔIN

SUSPENSE

Oh, hanging bridge across the gorge, you twine
Around existence ropes of twisted vine!

—BASHÔ

DESERTED

Quietness owns this hut without a host:
A woodpecker knocks on one veranda post.

—BASHÔ

TO HIS DISCIPLES

Since there's no rice for poets on the dole,
Let's do a flower arrangement in the bowl!

—BASHÔ

TOO EXUBERANT

Look where you're leaping, giddy crickets, you
Might land and split these emeralds of dew!

—ISSA

THE SCISSORS

A crane is screeching through the strident air:
Surely the broad banana-leaf will tear?

—BASHÔ

POETIC DESTRUCTION

A dragonfly: with finger-tip and thumb
Pull off its wings, and see—a capsicum!

—KIKAKU

"THAT IS NOT HAIKU!"

You take a scarlet pepper-pod, apply
Two wings of gauze, and look—a dragonfly![12]

—BASHÔ

CHAIN-MAIL

A chestnut dropped in. A goldfish rose to drink.
Their widening rings of water interlink.

—KIJIRÔ

THE PILGRIM

Without a word of warning, look, alone
Above the autumn clouds, Mount Fuji's cone!

—ONITSURA

THE HARVESTERS

Across the sun-scorched moorland, autumn passes;
Sparrows are hopping on the seeded grasses.

—SÔKYÛ

IN A CLIFF-EDGE FIELD

Shot by the scarecrow's aimless archery,
The harvest sparrows fall into the sea.

—SHIKI

GRISAILLE

The sunlit sea, when overcast for rain,
Is grey as driftwood with a silver grain.

—HÔ-ô

SEASIDE SKETCH

A gloomy downpour, pierced by shafts of light;
Out on the glittering sea, the sails are white.

—HÔ-ô

CRESCENTS

A new moon's silver fin ascends the dark,
As waves engulf the crescent-bladed shark.

—SHIDÔ

DURING MY ILLNESS

What majesty had Heaven's River, seen
Through windy holes worn in my paper screen!
—ISSA

CONSIDERATE

I must turn over, crickets, so beware
Of local earthquakes in the bed we share!
—ISSA

DOUBLE-EDGED

Into the darkness which a lightning-streak
Has slashed, recedes the wild night-heron's shriek.
—BASHÔ

MARINE

The midnight sky: an oyster-shell aswirl
With nacreous flakes of cloud; the moon—a pearl.
—HÔ-Ô

ON IZUMO CLIFF

Arching above the wild and gloomy sea,
Far out to Sado Isle—the Galaxy!
—BASHÔ

HIGH PERSIMMONS *by Ogawa Senô*

GLEANINGS *by Ogawa Usen*

PREAMBLE

Through morning mist, preceded by its moo,
The lowing cow looms slowly into view.
                                        —ISSA

THE BODHISATTVA'S NECKLACE

When from the moor the autumn mists have fled,
A spider's web has dew on every thread.
                                        —HAKUYÛ

TURN OF THE LEAF

The monk Ryôkan, whose tonsured stubble greys,
Feels sorry for himself on rainy days.
                                        —RYÔKAN

DEFIANT CREST

Only the cockscomb flaunts its curdled plume
Of purple seed amid the autumn gloom.
                                        —RANKÔ

ON THE DEATH OF THE POET ISSHÔ

Shake, O desolate grave-mound, shake! My wail
Of mourning is the autumn's headlong gale!
                                        —BASHÔ

DETACHED

The withered reeds break off, and day by day
Go drifting down the stream that flows away. . . .
—RANKÔ

SOUVENIR OF NARA

With ancient bronze Buddhas at Nara comes
The green, honeyed scent from chrysanthemums.
—BASHÔ

SKY CALLIGRAPHY

The wild geese write a verse against the glow
Over the hills; their seal—the moon below.
—BUSON

THE NEIGHBOUR

Autumn night on the river, with a moon;
My neighbour's flute is playing—out of tune!
—KÔYÔ

ENLIGHTENMENT

A water-rail's insistent cry has ended:
The broken moon among the reeds is mended.
—INAN

REVELATION

The gloomy stormclouds crumble, and behold!
The mountain in the moonlight, clear and cold.
                                        —BASHÔ

HIROSHIGE PRINT

An autumn moon looks round the mountain wall;
Maple-leaves chase the headlong waterfall.
                                        —HÔ-Ô

IGNORANCE

So whitely does the moon of autumn shine,
An owl seeks refuge in a wayside shrine.
                                        —JÔSÔ

THE CRIMSON CARPET

Scattered with maple-leaves where no one stepped,
My garden path is better left unswept.
                                        —HEKIGODÔ

AUTUMN SECLUSION

A single kiri-leaf falls, spiritless. . . .
Will you not come to me in my loneliness?[13]
                                        —BASHÔ

SINCE IT MUST BE SO . . .

You must remain. I must depart.
Two autumns falling in the heart.
                    —BUSON

INSPIRATION

The autumn wind: leaves patterning the air;
And for the poet, haiku everywhere!
                    —KYOSHI

THE WRECK

Here, in a puddle, recent rain has sunk
This upturned leaf: a beetle's yellow junk.
                    —HÔ-Ô

AUTUMN'S SENTINEL

Between the gates, where slanting sunset shone,
The mountain's shadow stretched—a stag thereon!
                    —BUSON

EVOCATIVE

Closing the temple's massive double gate,
Its hinges creak: the evening grows late.
                    —SHIKI

HOMECOMING AT SUNSET *by Nakamura Fusetsu*

EVENING ROOKERY *by Shibahara Kaizô*

UNSPOKEN

While willow-leaves continually fell,
My lord and I stood listening to the bell.
                    —BASHÔ

LAMENT

Autumn loneliness: a cricket grieves
This evening in the scarecrow's ragged sleeves.
                    —CHIGETSU

AT MYÔSHÔ TEMPLE

A garden from the past: as though of old
It wore the leaves' brocade of bronze and gold.
                    —BASHÔ

PERFECTION

The host said not a word. The guest was dumb.
And silent, too, the white chrysanthemum.
                    —RYÔTA

SACRILEGE

Before this perfect white inviolate
Chrysanthemum—the scissors hesitate!
                    —BUSON

THE GLOWING CAGE

Through scarlet maple-leaves, the western rays
Have set the finches' flitting wings ablaze.

—SHIKÔ

ON HER BETROTHAL

Is the persimmon hanging on the bough
Sweet or astringent? Take the marriage vow!

—CHIYO

SILENT TRAVELLER

The autumn sun goes down. Without a cry,
A crow has flown across the orange sky.

—KISHÛ

SECOND CHILDHOOD

We played at keeping house, a children's game;
Pretending—till the autumn sunset came.

—SHIKI

THE END OF AUTUMN

Autumn evening: on a withered bough,
A solitary crow is sitting now.

—BASHÔ

WINTER

MONOCHROME AT DAYBREAK

Against the chilly sky, washed grey with dawn,
A single pine-tree on the peak is drawn.

—GYÔDAI

CHALLENGE TO WINTER

Now let the frost with icy teeth devour:
Chrysanthemums are done, the last to flower.

—ÔEMARU

AMAZED

A temple on the hill: at break of day,
Its pounded bell startles the rooks away.

—YAYU

THE SECRET MEETING

Some water-fowl, and where the marsh begins
Among the withered trees: two palanquins.

—BUSON

ANOTHER WORLD

The teal duck surfaced: its astonished eyes
Fresh from the world that underwater lies.

—JÔSÔ

THE LONELY ONE

Ah, on the fallen leaves before my gate,
How far his footsteps sound for whom I wait!
—BUSON

LATE PERSIMMON

Wintry twigs: matured by frost and sun,
A globe of orange jelly hangs on one.
—HÔ-Ô

SOLAR KINSHIP

Swooping down to my gauntlet from the sky,
The sun is mirrored in the falcon's eye.
—TAIRO

INTERCHANGE

The sea: a silver flash without a sound;
But a dry surf of leaves along the ground.
—HÔ-Ô

THE GOLDEN EGG

Bare camphor branches, black against the west:
The sun is setting in an eagle's nest.
—BONCHÔ

AGAINST A WINTER SKY *by Ishikawa Kinichirô*

WILD DUCKS IN A CASTLE MOAT *by Shimomura Izan*

LIVING LEGEND

"Now long ago there lived a wicked witch . . ."
The withered pampas grass begins to twitch!
—ISSA

"EVERY DAY IS A GOOD DAY"

What happiness to wake, alive again,
Into this same grey world of winter rain!
—SHÔHA

THE NEW HAND

Straddling the turnip-top, I pulled with all
My strength—its root, ridiculously small!
—GINKÔ

CROSSING THE MOUNTAIN

Winter's first drizzle falls. The air is raw.
That shivering monkey needs a cape of straw.
—BASHÔ

ICY SURPRISE

A wintry blast: the mountain storm is here!
A hailstone skips into my horse's ear!
—TAIRO

UPDRAUGHT

The winds toss up into the stormy vault
The large white hailstones, where they somersault.
—SEKITEI

HOLIDAY

Look, children, hailstones hop about
And play at chasings! Let's run out!
—BASHÔ

FROST, THE MAGICIAN

The rime has frozen overnight to gems
Of crimson ice along the buckwheat stems.
—RANKÔ

THE ABSENT MOUNTAIN

Though veiled amid these misty showers of grey,
Fuji is lovelier still—unseen today.
—BASHÔ

CONTRARY-WILLED

Struggling to walk against this windy rain,
My wild umbrella drives me back again.
—SHISEI

IN ALL WEATHERS

Out on the moor, Jizô with shaven crown;
And from his nose an icicle drips down.[14]

—ISSA

THE ONLY TRACE

The travelling monk has vanished in the mists;
But still his little silver bell persists.

—MEISETSU

THE FINGER-POST

The farmer rose from where he dug and hoed:
A fresh-pulled turnip pointed out my road.

—ISSA

LAST POEM

Though on a journey I have fallen ill,
My dreams on withered moorland wander still. . . .[15]

—BASHÔ

BY THE OWARI SEA

Over foam-flecked waves in the falling night,
The wild ducks' cries are dying, dim and white.

—BASHÔ

SHADOW-SHOW

Two silhouettes upon the paper screen
Have melted into one: the night is keen.
— SEISETSU

AFTERWARDS

That rogue called Love has taken to his heels:
On snowy nights, how cold in bed it feels!
— JAKUSHI

SHARPENED BY THE COLD

A copper pheasant wakes with shrill-edged cry;
The silver crescent cuts the chilly sky.
— KIKAKU

WITH GETA ON

The footbridge, when I walked across alone
In winter moonlight, had a wooden tone.
— TAIGI

LAST FUGITIVES

Fleeing the wind, a few red maple-leaves
Cling to icicles pendant from the eaves.
— ITTÔ

人の顔のみかぶやのみ逢へる里の霜　冬城

FROST ON THE COUNTRYSIDE *by Honda Tôjô*

WINTRY GROVE UNDER A WANING MOON *by Sasaki Rimpû*

STREET-CRY IN WINTER

I call the old fishmonger back, but fail—
For he has disappeared in the pelting hail.
                              —BONCHÔ

COLD MEMENTO

A chill runs through the bedroom where I roam,
Treading by chance upon my dead wife's comb.
                              —BUSON

WINTER NANDINA

White with hoar-frost lies the garden bed,
On which one berry drops, a lively red.
                              —SHIKI

REACHING MII TEMPLE AT NIGHTFALL

At Mii's gate, the frozen bell was tolled:
Its shivering resonance increased the cold.
                              —ISSA

BESIDE THE TEMPLE GATE

The giant guardians stand in darkened stalls;
Their legs are bare, where icy moonlight falls.[16]
                              —ISSA

DESTITUTE

They take their only son, not ten years old,
To give the monks: a night of piercing cold.
—SHIKI

SAMSĀRA'S WHEEL

While the violent winter wind blows by,
One round moon rolls through the gloomy sky.
—MEISETSU

MONO NO AWARE

Ah! the first, the gentlest fall of snow:
Enough to make the jonquil-leaves bend low.
—BASHÔ

THE MONK IN THE WOODS

The winter's fitful gusts, as they expire,
Bring enough fallen leaves to build a fire.
—RYÔKAN

SOMETHING WONDERFUL

You kindle up a blaze; and then I'll show
You something wonderful: a ball of snow!
—BASHÔ

FRUGAL WINTER

Ash-smothered coals: and now at last it's hot,
The soup that simmers in the hermit's pot.
—BUSON

DEMONIC

How the boisterous howls of winter swell,
Pelting pebbles against the temple-bell!
—BUSON

THE VOID

Snow has obliterated all from sight:
Mountain and moor are now a world of white.
—JÔSÔ

LATE MIGRANTS

The storks are standing in a doubtful row,
Some on one leg, snow-white against the snow.
—KAKEI

ENVOI

The winter sun, rising with blood-red light
Behind them—ah, how rare and sad a sight![17]
—BASHÔ

WINTER RIBBON

A long black strand of river, far below,
Winds across the moorland, deep in snow.
                                    —BONCHÔ

GETA TRACKS

Morning snowscape: every wooden shoe
Has left imprinted there the figure two.[18]
                                    —SUTE (aged 6)

WEIGHT OF THE PAST

So deep the heavy snow since yesterday,
Its drifts remain—sweep, sweep as you may.
                                    —IZEMBÔ

THE VOICE OF SNOW

That flight of egrets, if they gave no cry,
Would be a streak of snow across the sky.
                                    —SÔKAN

CRYSTALLINE MIRACLE

Out of the air's spontaneous freezing grow
Delicate fretted hexagons of snow.
                                    —HÔ-Ô

BOY TRAVELLER IN SNOW *by Ôta Saburô*

SNOW DARUMA *by Kosugi Misei*

WHAT THE EAGLE SAW

Snowflakes falling through the air for miles
Above Shisaku's bay of pine-clad isles.

—HÔ-Ô

URGENT

Eleven horsemen riding through a night
Of swirling snow: none looks to left or right.

—SHIKI

HOSPITALITY

Denied a lodging for the night: the row
Of lights from houses standing in the snow.

—BUSON

THE OUTCAST

Disliked by all, refusing still to die
Even when weak with age: a winter fly!

—KIKAKU

A SAMURAI AT THE INN

Out of the flurried snow he entered; "Board
And bed!" he growled; and then flung down his sword.

—BUSON

LISTEN

Evening snowfall, with the faint dry crunch
Of straw that stabled horses twitch and munch.
—KYUKOKU

THE REAL CULPRIT

Hurry! Bring torches! Hurry, everyone,
And see the thief I've caught: my eldest son![19]
—SÔKAN

AT A MOUNTAIN RESORT

Snow-viewers climbing, one by one, from here,
Through falling veils of whiteness disappear.
—KATSURI

THE WORK OF MEN

Footprints have marred, in passing to and fro,
Pure perfection: the never-trodden snow.
—YAYU

THE NOTICE-BOARD

The snowy park invites; when I digress:
"No Admittance Except On Business."
—TOSHI

IN THE PARK

Snowfall at twilight: yet a mandarin drake
And duck still linger on the ancient lake.[20]

—SHIKI

THE UNKNOWN CALLER

"Yes, yes!" I answered, I'll be there anon."
But still my snow-piled gate was knocked upon.

—KYORAI

SUMI SKETCH

The branch is black and bare again: a crow
Shook down its coverlet of powdered snow.

—HÔ-ô

THE LIVING COLD

Winter seclusion: on the window-pane
The silver fern of frost has grown again.

—HÔ-ô

THE SMALL SAD SIGNS

The previous tenant's hardships, how he dwelt:
I know it all—even the cold he felt.

—ISSA

NOWHERE

One umbrella, as snowy dusk draws on,
Has come; and passes by; and now is gone. . . .
—YAHA

MAD WITH POETRY

Still with my one remaining tooth I bite
My frozen writing-brush that will not write.
—BUSON

CONVERSATION-PIECE

Though we have had the water boiling twice
For tea—our kettle wears a lid of ice!
—SÔKAN

THE WIND'S WHETSTONE

Through jagged cedars rips the winter blast,
Honed on the craggy ledges as it passed.
—BASHÔ

THE WOODCUTTER

Within the wintry grove, my axehead fell
And bit the bark—how startling was its smell!
—BUSON

CROWS ON BARE BRANCHES by *Suzuki Koson*

SAMPAN AND FALLING SNOW *by Nishi Ōshû*

WINTER AFFINITY

Where gnarled grey ropes of old wistaria-vine
Twist miserably: a temple in decline.
—BUSON

CHANGELINGS

The shifty foxes through the early hours
Of moonlight frisk among the jonquil-flowers.
—BUSON

DIMINUENDO

A waning moon sinks, fainter, into day;
Offshore, the plaintive plovers fade away. . . .
—CHORA

THE BROKEN RESOLUTION

Another year departs: the bell is tolled.
—And I intended never to grow old!
—JOKUN

LATE WINTER

So many white plum-petals fall and die:
Can it be spring already in the sky?
—HÔ-Ô

SIGNIFYING NOTHING

Between the washing-bowls at birth and death,
All that I uttered: what a waste of breath![21]

—ISSA

NEW YEAR'S DAY

On New Year's Day, the sky has cleared and leaves
Chattering sparrow-gossip in the eaves.

—RANSETSU

A PRISONER

Between the bars, the dove has stretched out one
Grey wing, to warm it in the winter sun.

—KYOKÔ

THE TWO PARAGONS

I would reserve Mount Fuji's peerless height
Of snow for New Year's Day—my only sight.[22]

—SÔKAN

THE THREE LOVELIEST THINGS

I have seen moon and blossoms; now I go
To view the last and loveliest: the snow.

—RIPPO (his death-poem)

ON HAIKU AND HAIGA: AN ESSAY

ON HAIKU AND HAIGA: AN ESSAY

SPIRIT AND SUBSTANCE

It is generally conceded that the artistic genius of the Japanese touches perfection in little things. Carved ivories for the girdle *(netsuke)*, metal-inlaid sword-guards *(tsuba)*, dwarfed trees *(bonsai)*, and other minor crafts—the exquisite workmanship and patient detail of these have won ready appreciation abroad. But on first encountering the poetry of Japan, the Western reader is often disappointed or puzzled to find that many of its greatest masterpieces are enshrined within that most diminutive of poetic forms: the haiku. For although, as he soon learns to his astonishment, the haiku is but seventeen syllables in length, at least four major poets have devoted their whole lives to composing nothing else.

Yet epic length is not necessarily an indication of poetic quality, however much the modern devotees of mass production and its "reign of quantity" may believe in the pseudo-gospel of statistics and worship sheer size. The huge or numerous is not always the great. To those discerning of spiritual values and the physical qualities consonant with them, one simple haiku by a master like Matsuo Bashô is worth more than a whole loudly acclaimed volume of verse with a merely contemporary appeal, just as a silk fan painted in monochrome by a Sesshû surpasses many a large canvas by some fashionable but ephemeral modernist. Thus many of the remarks made here apply equally well, *mutatis mutandis,* to the haiga, the haiku's pictorial counterpart, which is discussed in the following section.

Although in outer form so minute, the inner scope of the haiku may become immense in inverse ratio. As a nature

poem, its substance may be distilled into an intimate and tender miniature such as this, in which Bashô gives expression to what his countrymen call *mono no aware*—the "Ah!-ness of things," a feeling for natural loveliness tinged with sadness at its transience:

> Ah! the first, the gentlest fall of snow:
> Enough to make the jonquil-leaves bend low.

But from here its range may extend to a vision of the Japanese landscape on a vast scale, seen in the same poet's

> Arching above the wild and gloomy sea,
> Far out to Sado Isle—the Galaxy!

Within its tiny stanza, the haiku can hold such tragic intensity as Bashô's outburst "On the Death of the Poet Isshô":

> Shake, O desolate grave-mound, shake! My wail
> Of mourning is the autumn's headlong gale!

Or it may contain some deliciously whimsical exclamation, such as that by Buson, to which this book owes its title:

> What a delightful game it is to set
> Fireflies loose in bed beneath the net!

Again, it may release a dramatic but humorous surprise, as Kikaku does in this observation, so homely yet uproariously alive:

> A sudden downpour! Thunderclouds are cracking!
> And round the farmhouse all the ducks run, quacking!

With the minimum of "effects" but the maximum of effect, the haiku can evoke a romantic atmosphere, like that created by Môgan in

> The curtain of the daimyo's palanquin
> Was lifted. Cherry-petals drifted in.

But it can just as effectively deflate it with the pinprick of satire, as exemplified by Shiki's

> Autumn night on the river, with a moon;
> My neighbour's flute is playing—out of tune!

A whole tragic life-story or family chronicle, the germ of an unwritten novel or play, can be compressed into its narrow frame, as in this, again by Bashô:

> The household, standing by the ancestral graves,
> Are all white-haired and lean upon their staves.

While in as few words, it can reveal the comic view of life, as when Jakushi remarks with wry humour:

> That rogue called Love has taken to his heels:
> On snowy nights, how cold in bed it feels!

The haiku poet can turn inward upon our all-too-common human nature the same detached devotion with which he observes the passage of the seasons through the natural scene, and can smile with quiet penetration at his own failings, as Ryôkan does in his autobiographical yet objective

> The monk Ryôkan, whose tonsured stubble greys,
> Feels sorry for himself on rainy days.

How wonderful a medium the haiku may become for that ultimate simplicity which is so naive that it could only belong to man's second, and wiser, childhood is made apparent by Onitsura's world-shattering discovery:

> Again the cherry-buds are bursting through:
> Horses have four legs! Birds have only two!

It is doubtful if even Blake carried the childlike as far as this Japanese song of innocence. Only to sophisticates who have never entered the Kingdom of Heaven could this

appear to border on imbecility; for silly, indeed, it is—in the original meaning of that word.

Joining with this at the other extreme, the haiku in the hands of a master may hint at the metaphysical profundities of Mahāyāna Buddhist Doctrine, by making a few concrete images serve to exemplify the Universal Principles in which they participate:

> A water-rail's insistent cry has ended:
> The broken moon among the reeds is mended.

What, at first sight, seems no more than sensuous perception of nature, acquires, as we read between the lines, an added dimension from the hidden depths of *Śûnya,* the teeming Abyss of Infinite Possibility. The nightlong cry of the lake-bird obsesses the mind like *trishnā,* our thirst for life with never-to-be-satisfied craving and clinging. The full moon, in all those countries of the Far East to which the *Dharma* has spread, stands for the pure bright detachment of Buddhahood. To the Buddhist, it inevitably suggests the Clear Light of the Void, that Metacosmic Consciousness attained by Shakyamuni. Here, it is seen reflected in the dark lower waters of earthly existence; but only in fleeting and fragmentary gleams and glimpses. Such are the rare quicksilver flashes of *Prajñā,* the supra-individual Intuition, always immutably serene in itself, though apparently split and scattered on the agitated ripples of our distraction. But no sooner does the self-seeking bird cease to trouble these waters with its cry of unfulfilled desire, than the ever-calm lunar image of the Intellect comes together again, and our broken lights reintegrate within.

To the sensitive and cultured Oriental, who brings to the poem this tacit background of his Tradition, such a metaphysical interpretation is not merely an addition of painted legs to the live snake; it stings the poetry of the haiku to death as well. It should never have been made except to show the restless mind of our age, which in its onward impatience has no time to pause for contemplation and so no time for poetry, what unsuspected worlds may open up behind such simple and unassuming lines as these. We need but cultivate an inner ear for those overtones of meaning which the Hindu School of Manifestation, or Vyakti-vāda, regards as the soul of poetry, and has termed *dhvani,* "the reverberation of meaning arising by suggestion *(vyajñāna)*." Since it is inherent in Reality itself and accords with the changeless Principles, the sacred science of symbols requires no conscious contrivance of allegory. It is enough for it to exert its latent action of presence, without overt mention or explicit development, to give the poem its metaphysical dimension and spiritual resonance. These ideas find a Chinese parallel in the First Pictorial Canon of Hsieh Ho.

Sensing the Infinite and Eternal in the here and now, while always remaining free from philosophizing, the haiku can become the penultimate expression of the ultimately inexpressible. With delicacy and tact, it reveals to us the least, the most insignificant, of things as the Wholly-Enlightened One sees them through the compassionate eyes of Issa:

> O timid snail, by nature weak and lowly,
> Crawl up the cone of Fuji slowly, slowly. . . .

They are then seen to be infinitely precious and of eternal worth. The haiku's most halting and imperfect utterance can convey something of ineffable Perfection by its very incompleteness and inadequacy. Teishitsu, one of the earliest masters, is said to have composed no less than three

thousand haiku, only to destroy all but three, of which this is perhaps the most celebrated:

> I came to praise the cherry-blossom. "Oh! . . .
> Oh! . . ." That's all upon Mount Yoshino.

For tongue-tied eloquence this is excelled only by Ryôta's little masterpiece:

> The host said not a word. The guest was dumb.
> And silent, too, the white chrysanthemum.

This is the very same silence as that by which the Buddha, lifting up the lotus-bloom and smiling, communicated to Kaśyapa the Secret of Zen.

This briefest possible of verses is, in fact, not so much a poem, complete in itself, leaving room for nothing but admiration from outside, as a quintessentially condensed formula for a poetic experience: a *mantra* or verbal spell, potent yet refined, which will enable the reader, by imaginative collaboration with the words, to recreate in himself something of the poet's original moment of realization. By a few suggestive phrases, we bring that Vision to life again in our own experience, and so see things for once *yathâb-hûtam:* as they really are, freed from desire-impelled thought, in the ever-new light of that wonder which at every single moment recreates all the worlds.

Each true haiku is a swift record in words of one moment of *Satori,* of the sudden flash of Enlightenment which grants us a transcendent Insight into the Suchness of things. For one second, the Eye of Metaphysical Realization opens, and we are transformed into Buddhas. The next it closes, and we are forced to resume our separate and mortal selves again, imprisoned in the illusion of ordinary life. The full Enlightenment of a master demands an "every-minute

Zen," in which each unawakened moment of the mundane daily round would take on this illumined quality and merge into the continuous and unchanging blaze of *Bodhi*. This was the life dedicated to haiku, the life of *fûga* or poetic refinement, conceived and lived with a high measure of success by the tonsured layman Bashô, the Vimalakirti of Japanese poetry.

Just as in the *koan,* the nonsensical and solutionless problem used in Zen meditation, the period of paradox and puzzlement leads to a rational impasse and a blockage in our free flow of existence; so, too, in the haiku: just when every avenue of escape from the dead-ends of logic and the individual will seems closed or cut off, quite suddenly the instantaneous lightning of Satori flashes forth—and we see our way out. According to the *Abhidhamma,* or metaphysical section of the Pāli Canon, the longest process of consciousness caused by sense perception consists of seventeen thought-instants *(cittakkhana)* each briefer than a lightning-flash. Is it not significant in the light of this that a haiku should be composed of exactly seventeen syllables?

> I bowed before the Buddha, now obscure,
> Now bright with lightning, on the stormy moor.

This metanoiac shock, known to Sanskrit poetics as *samvegha,* has been treated by Ānanda Coomāraswāmy with his usual scholarly expertise and profound insight in an essay bearing that title in his *Figures of Speech or Figures of Thought?* Samvegha is at all times the unfailing sign and test of the presence of poetry, the essential seed of realization everywhere.

The spontaneous conception and impromptu expression required for a successful haiku are thus a supreme test of poetic concentration, conciseness, and clarity. The eye must

always be on the object: the poet nowhere to be seen. Yet the haiku should, like all genuine poetry, be multivalent, with reference simultaneously on all levels of being. Though it may merely state with the greatest economy of the *mot juste,* the auras of its words imply far more than what they state. The poem may be end-stopped, but its meanings must echo on. Like water-rings in a pool, their significances interlink and hint at what one should discover and develop for oneself. Thus the lover of poetry becomes a poet at second remove, and is led out of the poem altogether, directly back into the interdependent lives of bird and rock and tree.

Behind the simplest natural observation in haiku lies, as we have seen, the whole limitless universe of Zen, and by implication the vast intellectual superstructure of Mahāyāna metaphysics, which is its source. Even more: in his various stimulating works on Zen and haiku, R. H. Blyth lists among the artistic and spiritual origins and influences of this poetic tradition: Taoism, Confucianism, Shinto, Chinese and Japanese poetry and painting, and other indigenous arts and crafts such as the Noh drama, *ikebana* (flower arrangement) and *cha no yu* (tea ceremony). As he rightly affirms, haiku was to become the final channel for the deep cultural streams of the Orient, from India to Japan, distilling them all into a single bright drop.

When dealing with the influence of Zen on the arts and crafts in *The Way of Zen,* his latest and best book on Buddhism, Alan Watts devotes a few pages to the four moods, *sabi, wabi, aware,* and *yûgen,* which subtly permeate and flavour all Japanese culture. *Aware,* which he describes as "the moment of crisis between seeing the transience of the world with sorrow and regret, and seeing it as the very form of the Great Void," has already been illustrated. Since the other three moods are likewise too elusive and rarified to be defined, they can best be tasted by direct experience in the poetry itself.

Sabi, a poetic quality particularly stressed by Bashô, is felt in solitude; it is eternal "loneliness in the sense of Buddhist detachment, of seeing all things as happening 'by themselves' in miraculous spontaneity, a sense of deep illimitable quietude" as felt in one of the most famous and influential of haiku:

> Autumn evening: on a withered bough,
> A solitary crow is sitting now.

"The unexpected recognition of the faithful 'suchness' of very ordinary things" is how Watts characterizes *wabi;* to which he adds this example from Issa:

> I shut my brushwood gate; but should that fail
> To stop intruders, for a lock—this snail!

That haunting strangeness with intimations of Buddhist profundity which is the highest quality of the Noh theatre has been termed *yûgen* by Seami, its chief exponent and theorist. It is a never-to-be-fathomed mysteriousness, pervading such haiku as Bashô's

> Over foam-flecked waves in the falling night,
> The wild ducks' cries are dying, dim and white.

Again it must be insisted that there is little or no self-conscious symbolism or mythological personification, and almost no allegory at all, in this poetry of Tao and Zen.

> The white swan swimming to the shore beyond
> Parts with his breast the cherry-petalled pond.

This is not merely a piece of natural description, however lovely. But should the philosophically-minded be tempted to see in it a parable of the perfect detachment from the

passing beauty of this world with which the candidate for
Liberation makes his way to the Farther Shore, let him be
reassured that it is far more than that: it is a poem about
a white swan paddling through fallen blossoms on a pond!

The intellectual background is there—but never obvious
or obtrusive, never split off into a rationalized content—and
is all the better for being left unsaid. The sensuous perception does not symbolize the Metaphysical Principle in any
arbitrary or cerebral way: it *is* that principle manifest at
its own level in the hierarchy of Being. As the most transi-
tory swirl in the current of Becoming, it directly partici-
pates in the *Dharmadhātu,* the Archetypal World, as name
and form, in both its psychic and physical modes. Everything without exception possesses the Buddha-nature. The
last blade of grass has already attained Enlightenment;
but only the sages of Zen and the saints of haiku have as
yet reached the realization that the Diamond Sphere is
identical with this world of dew.

Although as a verbal formula, the final secret of the Buddhist Doctrine (Samsāra is Nirvāna and Nirvāna is Samsāra) is open and free for all to read; a natural esotericism
selectively veils its significance from all but those rare few
endowed with the spiritual qualifications and intellectual
capacities, whether innate or earned. It is these whose
attitude to existence unwittingly shows forth the authentic
spirit of Zen behind an often unprepossessing exterior. They
rest in compassionate non-attachment and yet display a
selfless courage. They delight in silence and solitude, ever
quietly contented amid loneliness and poverty. They radi-
ate an unconditional love for children and idiots and old
men, for animals and all other beings, sentient and non-
sentient, without discrimination. They give their insights
supra-rational expression through paradox, wordless action,

blasphemy, iconoclasm, and obscene humour. They extend a grateful welcome to whatever happens, living always in the present moment, without thought for the morrow. Their unquestioning acceptance of the everyday routine and rigours of monastic discipline, of ceaseless loss and change, of inevitable decay and death; the immediacy and directness of their every thought, word, and act, dealing only with the concrete, the objective, and the particular; their absolute freedom, even from the idea of being free, and above all from moralistic judgments; in a single phrase, their sublime simplicity—these are the principal qualities mentioned by Suzuki, Watts, Blyth, and others as characteristic of Zen method and attainment. And all will be found illustrated in the haiku here presented:

> The happy beggar, whom the passer loathes,
> Wears Earth and Heaven as his summer clothes.

To those who might wish to explore further the intimate relation between Zen and haiku, both as a poetic form and as a way of life, R. H. Blyth's *Zen in English Literature and Oriental Classics* may be strongly recommended as a lively and provocative revaluation of European literature, both prose and verse, from the standpoint of Zen. By showing how very little Zen indeed can be found in our literature, it effectively exposes our spiritual bankruptcy and sweeps away much dead and pretentiously moribund writing, though scarcely without some injustice done. Because of a failure to distinguish clearly between a Tradition in the religious mode, like Christianity, and one in the metaphysical mode, like Buddhism, some of Blyth's comparisons are odious and his incriminations misplaced. It is as pointless to look for Zen in the poems of Southwell as it would be to seek Catholic devotional mysticism in those of Hitomaro.

Some of our most notable scholars in this field do not seem to have realized that to translate the doctrines and ritual practices of the Mahāyāna Buddhist Tradition into those of Christianity is to denature both; since Buddhism, even in its Pure Land School, is not a religion. But despite a tendency to mistake personal dislikes and prejudices for detached insight, Blyth's heart is sound and full of light—and naturally on the right side!

FORM AND TECHNIQUE

Samvegha, the poetic shock, has been spoken of as the outward sign of the active presence of Satori in a haiku; and it is this moment of heightened awareness which also endows the haiku with its inner form as distinct from its verse pattern. The vertical spark of Insight into that Suchness whose whole is present in its every part, flashes instantly between two poles: Nirvāna and Samsāra. The "negative" pole is the infinite and eternal Void, which is too positive to be defined in any but negative terms. The "positive" pole is the finite and temporal Round of Existence, which is a merely negative deprivation from the viewpoint of the Indefinable. The former remains always the static and changeless Principle; the latter becomes its ever-moving and momentary application. Between these two, in that second during which we see the point of the haiku, travels the electric Intuition called *Prajñā*. This is well illustrated by Issa's startling verse on the Daibutsu at Nara:

> There sat the great bronze Buddha. From his hollow
> Nostril suddenly darted out—a swallow!

The immobile and monumental statue of the World-

Honoured One, who has been absorbed into timeless and spaceless Peace, is the perfect exemplar of the first term; while the swift and unexpected swoop of the swallow which, with nature's sublime disregard for limited human conceptions of the sacred, has built its nest in one of the colossal icon's nostrils, presents an equally apt example of the second. Their incongruous and unforeseen juxtaposition gives the authentic surprise of poetry, and expounds by an actual example the ultimate Buddhist revelation: Saṁsāra is Nirvāna. Each and every particular or aggregate of existence *is* the background of Non-Existence, one of whose infinite possibilities it realizes in manifestation. From that Unmanifest it "stands out" for one moment without duration; into that, in the very next moment, it is reabsorbed, to abide therein eternally as a unique *dharma,* reinstated in its permanent actuality. So, in Far Eastern paintings, do mountains, rocks, trees, rivers, and waterfalls emerge from mist-filled spaces of blank silk, define themselves in a few brief brush-strokes, and then are swallowed up once more in the omnipresent plenitude of Emptiness. Yet these, the final opposites, are in nowise opposed. Between them there can be no common measure, since the finite is rigorously nil when face to face with the Infinite. They are not One; and yet they are not two! Thus we see embodied in the occasional form of the haiku Bashô's dictum *Fû-eki ryûkô* or "Eternal truths in nature and human life expressed with freshness of technique."

Sometimes the penultimate extremes of One and Many are merely juxtaposed as in nature, and each must infer for himself their inner unity:

> The sun set on the swamp with orange glare;
> A ball of gnats revolving in the air.

In contrast to the Sun, Sphere of the Solar *Tathāgata,* Ma-

hāvairochana, and the perennial and imperishable Principle of Being, is set the ephemeral globe of tiny insect lives, representative of the five *skandhas,* or impermanent aggregates of Becoming, which even physically draw their vitality from that Life. The sheer contrast should be enough, without need to belabour the implicit symbolism.

Again, the lightning Vision may open up its vista between one line and the next, because of an abrupt shift from the microscopic to the macroscopic viewpoint, or the reverse:

> A seedling shoulders up some crumbs of ground:
> The fields are suddenly green for miles around.

Through the swinging doors of two adjacent seconds, the commonplace is seen from a strange angle in new patterns and colours, as when we look at the world standing on our heads—a thing which only children, fools, and yogis would be so naive as to do. But, suddenly, every day is the first day of creation, and once-upon-a-time is nowever.

One may, too, encounter strangely meaningful but almost ineffable correspondences between perceptions usually dismissed as unrelated: their "signatures" hinting sensuously at the Kegon School's concept of *jijimuge* or the mutual interpenetration of all existences:

> A new moon's silver fin ascends the dark,
> As waves engulf the crescent-bladed shark.

Anticlimax is the technical stratagem of others, which explode their subjects with an unanticipated deflation of the pompous and an affirmation of the real:

> My ears had found the sermon dull and stale;
> But in the woods outside—the nightingale!

Whereas St. Francis redundantly preached to the birds, the

Zen master Gensha reticently allowed a bird to preach in his stead.

Yet other haiku lift the humble and everyday toward the sublimely simple, disclosing the hidden qualities which link it uniquely to the Supreme:

> What majesty had Heaven's River, seen
> Through windy holes worn in my paper screen!

Skilled Chinese and Japanese potters can create a secret design by incising or embossing the clay before it is glazed with the same hue and fired; then, in a milk-white vase may be faintly discerned a bluish adumbration of some plum-blossoms floating on the crazed spring ice. Just so does the *haijin,* or composer of haiku, take pleasure in concealing in his verses a latent pattern of sight or sound.

> Beneath the bed's mosquito-net, I tie
> One corner up: the harvest moon is high.

says the poetess Chiyo. Although the casual or lazy reader, used to having his poets make all the imaginative effort, may see nothing much in this, the Japanese connoisseur at once recognizes a masterpiece. The source of his delight lies in the abstract geometrical pattern produced by the *square* of the mosquito-net, the *triangle* formed when one of its corners is tied up, and the *circle* of the full moon thus disclosed to view.

Perhaps more readily appreciable, since it finds a parallel in our own poetry, is a hidden pattern of sounds which echo the sense. Such meaningful onomatopoeia is to be heard in Kyorai's fascinating but never-to-be-resolved mystery of the unknown caller; where the four knocks on the wooden gate are repeated by the short "o" and "u" sounds in the translation (equivalent to the *tataku ya* of the Japanese):

"Yes, yes!" I answered, "I'll be there anon!"
But still my snow-piled gate was knocked upon.

Some haiku make no show of violence, nor do they attempt to take heaven by storm; rather, they allow their
poetry to dawn slowly on the reader, as in gradual enlightenment. They may be quiet to the point of pointless-
ness; so refined in taste as to seem tasteless, like the uniniti-
ated Westerner's first sip of steeped green tea. They require
a gentle repetition and contented familiarity before their
subtle flavour can be detected:

All day, with gently undulating swell,
The spring sea rose and fell, and rose and fell. . . .

Too obvious an observation to be thought worth recording
by any but a master like Buson, the effect here depends, in
both original and translation, on the *rhythmical* onomatopoeia, the technical principle of *shi-ori,* enunciated by
Bashô.

Sometimes it is not sound but silence that is conveyed
without verbal mention, but solely through its attendant
circumstances, described with rare and sensitive contrast
by Buson in his justly famous

A frail white butterfly, beneath the spell
Of noon, is sleeping on the huge bronze bell.

Using sound to express the soundless, few other poets
have ever caught, fleeting on the wing, the indefinable
atmosphere, the elusive spirit of place, which is sensed for
one moment only and then, like a faint perfume whose
source is unknown, evades all deliberate efforts at recapture:

The travelling monk has vanished in the mists;
But still his little silver bell persists.

Undoubtedly the quality which will prove most immediately striking to those previously unacquainted with the haiku is its pictorial definition of detail. Because its visual imagery is so immediate and vivid, drawn with such a swift economy of means, a haiku is the equivalent in words of the *sumi-e,* a rapid sketch in Chinese ink—a writing material, incidentally, which is erroneously named, being both solid and alkaline, whereas ink is liquid and acid. In a sumi drawing, a few spontaneously skilful touches imply, through the rhythmical gestures of the artist's hand and arm, the living movements of nature with which he is in contemplative union. Yet the painter adopts an almost abstract vocabulary of brushstrokes, each codified in the art manuals with a poetic name of its own. Thus every line and every area of tonal wash is an accepted visual convention, which can be "read," or recognized as subject-matter, by all who have learnt this art language. The technique may be acquired only after years of arduous practice, yet the final work be one of incomparable freshness.

> His brush abruptly leaps and flicks and swishes:
> Swiftly across the paper swim three fishes.

Much the same may be said of the haiku, whose subjects are often standardized, and whose vocabulary is not devoid of poetic diction: *samidare,* the summer monsoonal rains (rather than the modern *tsuyu); meigetsu,* the famous autumn moon; *hototogisu,* the onomatopoetic cuckoo with the conveniently five-syllabled name. These are derived from the poetic diction used in *waka,* or lyrical poems, during the Heian period, although haiku are fairly free from the stock epithet, or "pillow-word," which abounds in waka. But even after writing for several centuries on the set themes, poets can still manage to make fresh and moving observations of intense clarity and precision. No one could

deny the *hosomi* or exquisite nuance and delicate sensitivity
of Buson's

> An evening breeze across the reedy banks:
> Ripples around the blue-grey heron's shanks.

Even those who may not wish to go further towards
acquiring something of the cultural outlook of a Japanese,
necessary for deeper understanding, will at least be able to
appreciate such haiku as lovely miniatures.

Many haiku poets, indeed, have also been painters of
note, and have illustrated their own verses with rough but
vital sketches reduced to a minimum of strokes with the
writing-brush. These *haiga,* as such haiku paintings are
called, in no wise presume to be finished works of art.
Though less ambitious or detailed, they are rather the
counterpart in Japan of the impromptu album-paintings of
the Chinese literati, who regarded painting as one of the
accomplishments of a *chün-tzŭ* or Confucian gentleman, and
as an adjunct to the fine art of calligraphy, in which he was
an adept. Haiga are, however, sometimes crude and ama-
teurish—intentionally so—while their Chinese equivalents
are at worst uninspired and academic. Haiga are often intended to reinforce and supplement the impression made by
the haiku, translating simultaneously into two different
media the same poetic experience. But as may be seen in
those reproduced in this volume, many of which do not
even show the haiku that the painter would have had in
mind while painting, they may also stand alone as pictures
in their own right.

Sasaki Rimpû, in his postscript to the third volume of
the collection from which our haiga have been selected,
remarks that haiga should be drawn just as haiku are written: in a single breath, without thought or hesitation, and

with sparing touches of the brush. And so we may expect to find in haiga those same qualities which charm us in haiku. If, for instance, we turn to Pl. 5 (p. 22), by Nishi Ôshû, a strange and surprising juxtaposition of images confronts us: an *oni* or demon glaring at a violet. Yet what could sum up more aptly the unreconciled dichotomy in the Japanese temperament? Here is presented its paradoxical opposition of the demonic and the delicate, a supernatural rage and destructive glee face to face with a poetic sensitivity to the lovely and fragile growths of nature.

Haiga may also speak in similar symbolic undertones to their literary equivalent, as in Pl. 6 (p. 27), "Walking Alone in Spring" by Okano Sakae, where a subtle relationship may be seen between the drooping willow-boughs in first leaf and the dejection of the girl without a lover, the forward movement of her figure suggested by its diagonal slope.

Those haiku which capture a seasonal atmosphere or the spirit of a place can be paralleled by such haiga as Pl. 26 (p. 93), by Ishikawa Kinichirô, with its impressionistic treatment of a lord's cortege passing the shops in the village street and its evocative silhouette of palace roofs against the winter sky; while the quiet and gentle haiku finds its pictorial counterpart in Hirafuku Hyakusui's "Shy Rainbow" (page 54), where a first glance may miss the delicate hues of the arc demurely emerging after a shower, or the two birds perched among the wet leaves. The violence and drama of other haiku is matched by the weltering wind and torrential rain of the monsoon sweeping over the bamboos and thatched cottages in Shibahara Kaizô's "Sudden Downpour" (page 53), which has nicely placed and restrained touches of black and red amid its prevailing greys.

How appropriately might Yûki Somei's "Song of a Summer Shower" (page 48), with its lyrical treatment of bird

and rain and its masterly use of "broken ink" technique in petals and leaves, stand as an illustration to Bashô's haiku "With Sharpened Senses" (page 40); or Nakamura Fusetsu's "Plum-blossoms"(page 15) receive as its poetic inscription the haiku by Sodô with which this book begins. The poet, contemplating through his moon-window the first plum-blossoms bursting forth from a gnarled old stump, distills the quintessence of spring, and the white voids in figure and background hint at that No-Thing which contains everything.

The comic economy and childlike simplicity of haiku are to be observed again in the little dog with curly tail, reduced in Ogawa Senô's deft rendering to the ultimate minimum of lines, as he looks up expectantly while his master is knocking down the persimmons out of reach in Pl. 22 (p. 79). The naive spirit of the true haiku tradition informs the snowman in the likeness of the fierce and legless Daruma, founder of the Zen School in China, who stands under a half moon amid black clouds (page 106); as well as the sampan on a frozen river in the falling snow rendered by dabs of white paint straight from the tube (page 112).

It may be that those who have come to expect the technical accomplishment of a trained artist will be disappointed and deterred by the apparent crudeness of such unprofessional sketches by the poets themselves. But as the haiku painter Otsuji wisely points out in his colophon to the fourth volume of the *Gendai Haiga Shû,* "The mystery of haiga lies in its clumsiness. If drawn with a vigorous spirit, a sublime beauty shows through the very gaucheness of the picture." As an example of this, "High Clouds at Noon" by Ogawa Senô (page 41) will amply support his view. Who would have thought that the whole of a summer's day, with its white cumulus clouds soaring above the flowering moor, could have been evoked by so few casual and careless strokes?

Not that skill with the brush is lacking in these spontaneous paintings: note how the simplified curves and pastel colours of Pl. 12 (p. 47), "Bath in Summer" by Ôta Saburô, capture the femininity of the figure and catch her typical gesture as she washes under her arm; how cunningly delineated are the geta; how controlled yet free the touches of pale contrasting green in the grass-blades.

Just as in some haiku, puzzlement precedes realization, so in a haiga like Pl. 25 (p. 86), the eye sees at first only an almost abstract pattern of lines, shapes, and colours; but later, when these suddenly come together and cohere, the viewer realizes with delight that they represent a colony of crows with large pointed beaks, who have perched in characteristic attitudes on branches above the brown rice-stubble.

Between the haiga and the haiku that is sometimes inscribed on it there often appears to be an intimate yet intangible affinity; as when the cursive "grass" characters of Pl. 3 (p. 16) suggest the upward push and uncurling growth of young shoots in spring; or when the erratic calligraphy of Pl. 9 (p. 34) echoes visually the fluttering fall of the cherry-petals and, like them, contrasts with the bold circular brush-sweep in the parasol. Here both picture and script seem to embody the same rhythmic vitality. Less often, the haiga needs the inscribed haiku for its full comprehension, as in Pl. 16 (p. 59), where only the words make it clear that the Buddhist pilgrims are listening to a rainstorm of cicada-song which fills the whole mountain after heavy rain.

But in all haiku and haiku painting, economy, understatement, and omission remain master principles, exemplified by the summary treatment of hill and sunset in Pl. 24 (p. 85), by Nakamura Fusetsu, and by the ambling two-

year-old horse descending a slope which there is no need for the artist to depict at all.

One at least of the greatest writers of haiku, Buson, was equally talented and renowned as a professional artist. That "his pictures were poems and his poems pictures," as was said of Wang Wei, should be evident from those already quoted. Some haijin even went so far as to substitute in their script small pictures of objects for the words which refer to them: a little drawing of Mount Fuji, for example, being incorporated into the verse instead of the written characters. In the Far East, where for centuries painting has been formally considered as a branch of calligraphy, this procedure is less eccentric and strange than it would appear with us, especially when one remembers the pictographic origin of the Chinese characters. But it still remains rather rare, and as a rule, the possibilities of the two media are kept distinct though parallel, even when the poem is inscribed on the accompanying picture.

Both haiku and haiga possess the same choice observation of nature. Each translates it through a different artistic language with spiritual immediacy and selfless skill, achieved only after decades of Zen-like training in contemplation and technique, until the artist has reached the state of "No-Mind" *(wu hsin)*. This is a plane of mental relaxation and manual dexterity, only to be attained by the most laborious discipline and repetitious practice, whereby all illusion of an individual ego is eliminated. Tao can then take control and work through the artist's hand and eye, which it does infallibly, performing the miracle of manifestation without the slightest effort, once the obstructions and distractions of thought are removed. If the human mind does not meddle, there can be no muddle. But on no account should this superconscious state be confused, in the manner of the Freudian and Jungian analysts, with that subconscious swamp through which the surrealists flounder and are lost, to founder at last in insanity. Their psycho-pathological outpourings are the inverse image of the spiritual world, a realization of the most inferior residues of the soul. The isolated ego may very well be "unconscious" that it is even now in the hell of Avīchi; it may even be induced to mistake a technological nightmare for the Earthly Paradise. But however carefully it may be insulated by the propaganda of the modern "life-cult" from both Heaven and Hell, they are not therefore the same place.

The rational self-will explores every possible way out of its existential impasse until, its presumption exasperated and its powers exhausted, the poet is finally forced to admit his utter impotence to create. In the problem's own terms, no solution can be found by using the merely in-dividual faculties. There is simply no effective course of action by which to extricate oneself. Nothing relevant whatsoever can be done. But if failure can be faced without despair, then, quite suddenly, the ego will relax its clinging grip on life—and behold! Tao presents the poet with the only perfect and possible solution: one so simple, so inevitable, so economical, yet so elegant. He finds that it has been lying, self-evident all along, under his very gaze. Only the imbecile "I" could have failed to see and to seize upon it right from the beginning. This is known to be so, not only from the author's experience, but also from an examination of the tentative drafts of haiku left behind by the great haijin, in which we see them fumbling clumsily before trial and error finally gave way to the perfectly crystallized form, which emerged always in a timeless moment of more-than-human skill. Yet without the initial inertia, without the mental blockage and the emotional

battle, no answer from the teeming Void would ever seem to be forthcoming, no gift of grace or insight freely and unconditionally given. Man's extremity is Tao's opportunity. Śūnyatā sells all good things to us at the price of labour. But it is not by self-effort or social compulsion that they are created. Such ignorant labours serve only to prove the vanity of human aspirations to increase one's spiritual stature by taking thought. After circling aimlessly on Saṁsāra's Wheel of Flux, by which we arrive nowhere; after being caught up in the endless Round of action and reaction, only to find ourselves back where we began; all at once, the discrete leap in the dark is made from the circumference of Becoming to the centre of Being, from the never-ceasing revolution of the rim, to the still hub of contemplation. Mind has been used to transcend itself and to arrive at No-Mind. It has disappeared into the creative gap between two thoughts.

Most of us are intent on making a career of our limitations. Our lives are spent forever standing in our own Light. Our darkness-loving thought, unable to endure the white glare of pure Consciousness, retreats to the external forms of Tradition, its symbols and ritual, its doctrines and institutions, as in the well-known formula "I take refuge in the Buddha, the Dharma, and the Sangha." The haiku poet expresses it much more economically and integrally, without the dichotomy of reason:

> So whitely does the moon of autumn shine,
> An owl seeks refuge in a wayside shrine.

But habitual action, the automatism of Karma which obsesses and compels, is the great obstruction to the sudden shining forth of Consciousness, the Moon of Buddhahood which always glows within. This is so because heightened awareness arises at the moment of meeting between action and inaction, at which point is manifested the *wu wei*, or actionless activity, of the Taoists. Even the faint light of our selfish consciousness, remotest reflection of that Lunar Sphere, is produced by the encounter of excitation and inhibition. The name arouses us to action in regard to the form; but as words are fingers pointing to the Moon, and not the Moon itself, we stand baulked on the very brink of action. We are left poised in mid-act, with a thrilling sense of being-just-about-to. Yet it is in this momentary pause that we have the opportunity to pass through the portals of the Supernal Sun and be blinded by Reality. Poetic realization gives us as much as we can stand of Liberation while still in love with our chains.

Some salient detail is chosen by the haiku poet and embodied in the fewest and liveliest words. Our attention remains balanced for one instant on that point, like a quicksilver drop on a nasturtium leaf, before it runs off, and we are hurried on by practical necessity to read the next phrase. Already there is high and subtle artistry in the poetic power of selection; as when Buson represents the human friends by their two most striking attributes only:

> Through this shower in spring, at dusk dispersing,
> A raincoat and umbrella stroll, conversing. . . .

To detain us longer, the poet may compare his chosen detail with another, similar as sheer experience, but of no practical use, thus inviting us to savour its pure quality. In this way, onward action is delayed, and we perceive a splendour in the grass. The bud of pure consciousness can flower in that one moment of contemplative respite from the Round.

> This butterfly which on a poppy clings
> Opens and shuts a booklet's paper wings.

Max Eastman has expounded, psychologically and physio-logically, this theory of the withholding of action and the arousing of awareness; but it lies at the metaphysical basis of Oriental culture with much more profound significance than he suspected. "Awaken the mind without fixing it anywhere," says the *Diamond-Cutting Sutra,* on first hearing which, the illiterate wood-gatherer Hui Nêng at once at-tained Enlightenment, and became the father of Chinese Zen. These words contain the quintessence of the whole Buddhist method. Outward action is stilled, and inward activity stimulated, until a crisis is reached, and both cease and are transcended. Or, since while yet alive all must act, the outer action is performed in utter tranquility and detachment from the selfish desire for fruits. Be still, and know that you are the Buddha. It is for this that Zen monks sit for long hours in *zazen,* cultivating consciousness. For this they worry over a koan, which by its very paradox and absurdity exasperates the will to succeed and frustrates all action, both psychological and physical, until the ego gives up the struggle: pure Consciousness immediately floods the whole being with Light, and once more we have become what we always are. To sip a haiku to the full is to have a brief foretaste of the nectar of Nirvāna.

Whereas most very short poems in European languages are epigrammatic in character and intention, few haiku fall into this class; so that the "Japanese epigram," as Chamber-lain called it, is a misnomer; unless, as sometimes happens, the verse is quite literally "written on" a fan or album-leaf. Some of Kikaku's haiku approach the Western epi-gram:

> Disliked by all, refusing still to die
> Even when weak with age: a winter fly!

As such, they are farther from the true haiku as defined by Bashô and closer to *senryû,* one of those satirical poems which use the same verse form, but whose themes are human faults and foibles in humorous or discreditable social situations. Like its pictorial counterpart, the *ukiyo-e,* or colour woodblock print of eighteenth-century Edo, the senryû is considered rather vulgar by the most refined Japanese taste, though it is, of course, generally preferred by Europeans with their anthropocentric outlook. A still closer parallel would be with the satirical sketches, often drawn with a single continuous line, which Hokusai included in his *Manga* (a generous selection from which is beautifully reproduced in James A. Michener's recently published *The Hokusai Sketchbooks);* while the haiku, on the other hand, bears more resemblance to the classical woodcuts of the Kyoto School.

Much of Kikaku, Bashô's naughty left-hand disciple, is balanced precariously on the brink between haiku and senryû. As the founder of the Edo-za or Tokyo School of haiku-writing, Kikaku might also be regarded as the spiritual father of senryû, as shown in such haiku as this:

> Dreaming of battles, was I slain in fight?
> I'm peppered with rosettes: those fleas can bite!

The eponymous founder of the form, however, was Karai Hachiemon (1718–90), from whose literary name of Senryû ("River Willow") this poetic genre derives.

What most distinguishes the two is that whereas the senryû is an epigram on the aberrations and absurdities of humanity, the haiku is an extremely condensed recipe for a nature poem, though not exclusive of human nature. Every haiku is required to contain a seasonal reference *(kisetsu),* some word or phrase which will establish the

time of the year, though not necessarily the name of the season *(ki)*. By a long-standing poetic convention, there are certain creatures or climatic changes which can perform this function, such as the *uguisu* or Japanese nightingale, which arrives in the spring and sings in the daytime; or *kareno,* the withered moor, indicative of early winter. A list of the most important kisetsu or season-words, which also provide the commonest themes for haiku, is given by Asatarô Miyamori in his monumental *Anthology of Haiku, Ancient and Modern* as follows:

"*Spring:* (February, March and April) Springtime, Haze, Snow left unmelted, Spring rain, the Spring moon, the *Uguisu* or Japanese nightingale, which is the sweetest bird of passage, Larks, Swallows, Butterflies, Frogs whose songs *(not* croaking) are appreciated by Japanese poets, Cherry-blossoms which are the most beautiful of Japanese flowers and so highly appreciated that when the *haijin* simply mentions 'the flower,' he means the cherry-flower, Plum-blossoms which are considered the next best flowers, Violets, Willows, Camellias, Peach-blossoms, Wistaria, Peonies, Azaleas.

"*Summer:* (May, June and July) Summertime, *Koromogae* or 'Changing Clothes' (In Old Japan on the first of April of the lunar calendar, i.e. about May of the solar calendar, spring suits were changed for summer ones), the May rains (In May of the lunar calendar, i.e. June of the solar calendar, it rains for some three weeks in succession), *Yûsuzumi,* or 'Enjoying the cool evening breeze,' Cuckoos, Fireflies, Cicadas, Goldfish, Dragonflies, Morning-glories, Lotus-flowers, Poppy-flowers, Summer chrysanthemums, Lilies.

"*Autumn:* (August, September and October) Autumn evenings, the Milky Way, the Harvest moon (The best full moon of August 15th of the lunar calendar or of September 22 or 23 of the solar calendar; the harvest moon is so highly appreciated that when the *haijin* says simply 'the moon,' 'to-night's moon,' *meigetsu* (the famous moon) or 'the bright moon,' he means the harvest moon) Wild geese, Crows, Woodpeckers, Quails, Insects (several insects whose sweet notes are highly esteemed), Chrysanthemums, Maple-leaves and all other trees whose leaves turn scarlet, Scarecrows, Paulownias, Ivy.

"*Winter:* (November, December and January) Winter, Falling leaves, Frost, Ice, Hail, Snow, the Winter moon, Withered fields, the Close of the year, New Year's Eve, Camellias, New Year's Day, Mandarin ducks."

Professor Blyth in his comprehensive and carefully annotated collection of haiku in four volumes gives an even more specifically detailed classification under numerous subheadings for each season.

For its outer form, or principle of versification, the haiku, as is well-known, employs neither rhyme nor metre, whether quantitative, inflected, or accentual. It is distinguished from prose only by its poetic diction, its melody of assonance and alliteration, often with onomatopoeia, and its division into three lines, so arranged as to have a count of five, seven, and five syllables respectively. Haiku rhythm on the other hand, as distinct from metre, is determined by vowel quantity, where the long vowels are considered to be twice the length of the short ones, and by the slight inflection in pitch of the voice as required by meaning or expressiveness.

A haiku is really the first section of a waka or tanka, where it is rounded off by two seven-syllable lines, making thirty-one in all. The haiku is first found separated from the

concluding fourteen syllables during the fourteenth century in the *Tsukuba Collection,* an anthology compiled by Nijo Yoshimoto (1320–88). From about the beginning of the Christian era, short linked poems, or tanka, were composed by two poets in collaboration, the first improvising the triplet, and the second capping it with the couplet. Long linked poems, involving a sequence of such tanka began to appear, according to Blyth, somewhere in the later part of the Heian period (794–858). "In the early part of the Kamakura Era (1186–1339)," he remarks, "such linked poems became exceedingly popular, and two schools arose: the serious, *Ushina,* and the comic, *Mushina.* The Mushina gave the name of *haikai renga,* 'Sportive Linked Poems,' abbreviated to haikai, to their compositions, and this came to be used of all such poetry and poetic exercises. The word haiku is a mixture of this expression, haikai, and *hokku,* the first part of the Long Linked Verses; haikai plus hokku becoming haiku about the middle of the 18th Century." Since about the same period, *haikai* or *renga* have been called *renku.* Such renku, or impromptu linked verses, the result of a collaboration between a master-poet as leader and one or more players at a poetry-making party, reached the height of their popularity in the Muromachi period (1392–1490). It was still practised with occasional conspicuous success by Bashô and his disciples in the seventeenth century, but since that time has gradually died out for want of a galaxy of contemporaneous talent. In spite of elaborate rules, the renga is loose and inconsequential in structure, since only adjacent verses are related in subject and season, and insufficiently so to make it the poetic equivalent of the long landscape-roll in painting.

It was, then, from such playful and artificial origins that the profound art of haiku took its rise. Fuller descriptions of its historical development are presented by Miyamori, Blyth, and Yasuda, and a shorter account for the general reader is the chapter on poetry in *Japanese Literature* by Donald Keene. It would be redundant to retrace here the history of haiku writing, even in outline; or to offer biographies, however brief, of the chief haijin; since this ground has been thoroughly covered by the various works mentioned in the bibliography. Miyamori gives the lives of the four greatest masters of haiku, along with some of their sayings on the art. These latter may prove refreshing to those Western poets who have grown weary of the now superstitious cult of contemporaneity.

PRINCIPLES AND PROBLEMS OF TRANSLATION

Nothing, as René Guénon rightly affirmed, could be more misleading or open to grosser misunderstanding than a literal translation from an Oriental language into a European one, especially when presented bare of interpretative notes or those oral explanations from a master which would invariably have accompanied it in the East. Rather, if the spirit of the original work is to be caught and its meaning carried over into the foreign tongue, should that other principle enunciated by Guénon be constantly borne in mind: the translation must correspond to a commentary written in the original language. His own works are models of how such adaptations, which always adhere strictly to the doctrines translated, ought to be made for the Western reader.

Yet such is the modern obsession with mere facts, that is to say with the most superficial effects and appearances, that the literary critic no longer asks whether the translation is

true to the inner content of the text, at each of the four levels named and analysed by Dante: the literal and narrative, the social and political, the philosophical and theological, and the esoteric and initiatic. His only demand is that the version be literal—as if that were in itself a guarantee of faithfulness; and as though most of our errors and ignorance in the past were not due to taking literally what was meant figuratively. Needless to add that, with his outlook and judgment limited to the "aesthetic surfaces," the critic considers the multiple truth of the poet's matter to be little or no concern of his, and of importance only in so far as it supplies the occasion for the poet's manner, which is to be enjoyed for its own sake. He need but suspend his disbelief in the poetic thesis for the duration of the work in order to admire its stylistic effects as literature. What matter that the poet devoted his whole life to the communication of his meaning? His display of talent is a mere entertainment, a higher-class circus. Thus the literary means are mistaken for the end; indeed, are made into an end in themselves. Then, as Ānanda Coomāraswāmy never tired of reiterating (though far from unnecessarily, since few have as yet heeded his words), figures of thought decline into figures of speech; and the private fantasies of the poet who "expresses himself" replace the universal language of the mythopoetic Imagination, expressive channel for the Creative Spirit, which, in the "selfless, Self-absorbed delight of art," alone is present. Coomāraswāmy's devastating criticisms, which completely demolish our morbid and moribund modernism, are obviously too uncomfortable to attract much attention. There are certain sinister interests, both psychological and social, which do not wish to know that the basic fallacies of their position have been undermined in advance.

In these days, when the standards of poetic craftsmanship have sunk to their lowest level, almost any word-for-word version needs only to be printed in lines to pass for a "verse" translation. Deprived of any traditional standards and conditioned by fashionable and influential critics, readers are now prepared to accept a line-by-line rendering in what could in no wise be dignified with the noble name of prose, let alone that of poetry. They no longer dare to assert their rights and demand of the translator that he make some attempt at reproducing the rhyme and rhythm, the stanza pattern and verbal music of the original, and that, above all, the result be English poetry. When any attempt to sacrifice the letter to the spirit is likely to be denounced or dismissed out of hand, it becomes necessary to offer some apology for a verse translation which aims not at the modern obsession of literalness, but at formal qualities and poetic liveliness.

It has long been recognized that the central problem in the translation of poetry is the re-creation in one's own tongue of a poem parallel to that in the foreign language. Such poetic realizations of the same theme in an equivalent style have perforce been very rare, for not only have few poets interested themselves in traditions other than their own, or had the patience and perseverance to spend arduous years acquiring an Asiatic tongue, merely to transplant other men's flowers; still fewer have been those proficient linguists who were also poets, or were equipped with even a minimal technique in versification. If these qualifications are seldom to be found combined in the one person, the obvious solution is a collaboration between the taste and talent of the poet and the linguistic competence of the scholar. These prerequisites, of course, are slight compared with what is demanded of one who in the East would

aspire to the title of translator; as those who have read
Marco Pallis's admirable account in *Peaks and Lamas* will
already know. There is another essential in the equipment
of a translator of Oriental texts that is as necessary as poetic
ability, a knowledge of the culture and ethos, and sensibility and skill in handling two widely different idioms: this
is the need for some practice in Eastern methods of contemplation, the Yoga of poetry, without which the translator, no matter how learned, cannot hope to reconstruct,
even approximately, the original poet's experience, and so
transmit both subject and spirit to us. He must have infused
into his re-creation a vision and a vitality approaching that
of its creator if the poetry is to survive transplantation. And
he can only do this if he has stepped outside the limitations
and prejudices of his own culture, and placed himself within
the framework of the Oriental one, steeping himself with
intuitive understanding in its wisdom and faithfully practis-
ing its methods, until this new spiritual outlook is no longer
exotic, but as natural as his own. It is worse than useless
for him to approach his subject of study as a sceptical or
partisan outsider, tacitly convinced of the presuppositions
of his own period.

In these poetic paraphrases, therefore, it has been made
an ideal rule of composition that each had to be conceived
and expressed only after long contemplation of both the
original and its various former translations. The meaning
and imagery were held poised in imagination until fully
and freshly realized. Then, and then only, could each haiku
re-emerge spontaneously, clothed in English words and
rhythms which would preserve and communicate its inner
life as intact as possible. If inspiration presides, then minor
departures and variations in wording are of small account.
The final form of expression had to spring to mind in one

of those immediate moments of No-Mind, one of those "golden hunches" which are poetic Satori. But since during that moment no one is present to own the authorship, naturally no personal claim is made here that all of these versions are equally successful or attain any high degree of perfection.

Unfortunately, most haiku translations in the past have been undertaken by scholars who were not also poets and, what is worse, were temperamentally out of tune with Zen. Since Chamberlain's pioneer work on Japanese poetry appeared in the 1880's, containing a chapter on "Bashô and the Japanese Epigram," which was probably the first attempt to render haiku into English, there have been a fair number of translations; so the student can now profit from the linguistic spadework of a long line of predecessors, which includes Chamberlain, Porter, Page, Noguchi, Miyamori, Yasuda, Henderson, Blyth, and others. Although some of these translations show intermittent flashes of poetry and occasional felicities of phrase, most of them fall far too often into old-fashioned "poetic" diction and rhetoric, prosaic flatness, and a sentence structure determined by exigencies of metre and rhyme. The haiku is, after all, a Japanese *poem:* it is neither three lines of unrhythmical prose, as even the versions of Blyth (in many ways the best) would lead an English reader to suppose; nor is it an exercise in the clichés of poetic sentiment, couched in archaic diction and syntactical inversion, as earlier translators presented it, unaware that their poetic licences had long since expired.

William N. Porter seems to have been the first to try out a three-line stanza, whose first and third lines, containing two or three stresses, rhymed, while its middle line, of three or four stresses, was left blank. With few exceptions,

his versions are conventional and pedestrian, often as far from the originals in letter as in life, and worst of all, quite devoid of Zen. Henderson also adopted this form, and achieved some neatly turned and notable successes with it; but it has never really become acclimatized as an English stanza. Though Henderson's are perhaps the best of the verse translations hitherto, this form betrays him from time to time into unnatural rhyme-induced distortions of syntax, not to mention such bathetic dialect-diction as: "little gossoons," where the Japanese simply says "children"; "snail, my little man"—a most unoriental anthropomorphism to gain a false rhyme with "Fujisan"; and "The tower high I climb," which, apart from the inversion and the three long "i" sounds, is surely the phrase outmoded. It offers, too, an instructive instance of a failure to evoke in the mind's eye of a European the visual image which would immediately offer itself to that of a Japanese. To achieve this, it would be necessary to write "pagoda" and not just "tower," this most probably being the kind of tower intended by the poet, who has ascended it in spring in accordance with Far Eastern custom. Page is likewise guilty of gross lapses of taste in his attempts to be coy, whimsical, or petite, sometimes expanding his overstatements to many times the length of the Japanese and giving away the whole point of the haiku. Asatarô Miyamori, whose *Anthology of Haiku, Ancient and Modern* contains some pertinent criticisms of the failure of previous translators in the West to grasp even the overt sense of many haiku, due to their unfamiliarity with Japanese culture, is himself defeated by an Oriental's understandable lack of feeling for what is acceptable in modern English poetic diction. Thus, innocently unaware, he can offer as serious translation lines containing such archaisms as in the following, which his considerable reading in the masters of English literature of past centuries has led him to believe are still "poetic":

> "Life is the morning dew, bards say;
> 'Tis true indeed, but well-a-day!"

None of these verses, though they occasionally rise to poetry, can in any way be claimed as the original work of their translators, who received their moment of re-inspiration in the first place from the great haiku poets. Since in translations, as in ideas, there can be no such thing as private property, little hesitation has been shown in adopting or adapting whatever could not have been better expressed; not, of course, for any personal glorification, but solely for that of the original poet, whose genius alone all are committed to serve and to honour with a translation as felicitous in the letter and faithful in the spirit as several minds can make it. Thus these haiku in English couplets, a form first used by Professor Miyamori, really represent a collaboration between a poet and a tradition of translators, through whom an ever-deepening understanding can be traced, from the white superiority of a Chamberlain, attracted in spite of his prejudices, to the profound insight of Blyth, an indispensable guide, who has himself studied in Zen monasteries in Korea and Japan.

From what has already been said, it should by now be apparent why, in as elusive and elliptical a language as Japanese, a verse translation *au pied de la lettre* is simply out of the question without betraying both poetry and import. Learned allusions to Chinese classical literature and culture, exclusively Japanese idioms, serious puns, and untranslatable "pivot-words," not to mention the extreme condensation and at the same time often colloquial indefiniteness of

grammar and syntax, along with widely differing resources of vocabulary—these make paraphrase in most haiku almost inevitable if the results are not to prove unintentionally comic.

As an example of the problems facing the translator of haiku may be cited the *kireji* or "cutting-words," which are such a feature of this form. The kireji is an exclamation marking the threefold division of the theme into subject, time, and place, as well as a pause in the rhythmic flow. It usually cuts the verse after the first five syllables, but it is often to be found at the end of the seven-syllable line, and more rarely its appearance is recognized as possible at the conclusion of the whole haiku. Of these cutting-words, four are most frequently met with: *ya, kana, keri,* and *yara,* which according to Henderson can be approximately rendered as follows:

ya: Lo! Behold! or other exclamations directing attention.
kana: Ah!—a sigh.
keri: serving to intensify the verb.
yara: the feeling of a question to which no answer is expected.

As too free and frequent a use of such interjections as Oh! Ah! Lo! and Behold! is likely to induce a faint vertigo in the reader, a punctuation mark has often to do service for one of the kireji.

Japanese being a language rich in homophones, *engo,* which are associated words and syllables of identical or similar sound but of different sense, largely take the place of our poetic figures; so another sore puzzle for the translator is the serious pun, along with its relation the *kake-kotoba* or "pivot-word." Rippo has a death-bed haiku on

"The Three Loveliest Things" (which the Japanese consider to be the moon, cherry-blossoms, and snow):

> I have seen moon and blossoms; now I go
> To view the last and loveliest: the snow.

The word *yuki,* meaning "snow," has as one of its homophones another word *yuki* which signifies "going" and refers to the poet's imminent departure from this world. The Japanese have the saying *"Yuki no hate wa Nehan"* (After the snow comes Nirvāna), and so because the snow symbolizes not only the cold of death but also the purity of the Void, Śūnya, whose dazzling whiteness is devoid of all distinctions, and because the dying poet hopes to attain to that state, a latent association with a third possible homophone, *yuki* meaning " auspicious," may be aroused. By a masterly understatement, this key word is not mentioned in the poem at all, being alluded to merely as the third of the triad of beautiful things.

Such serious puns are not altogether unknown in our literature: Shakespeare used them, even at the height of tragedy. But it is very rarely that they can be rendered directly or exact equivalents found for them in English. Most are quite untranslatable without lengthy explanation, and usually they must be expanded into a simile or implied by a metaphor.

Often the two halves of the Japanese verse turn upon a *kake-kotoba* or pivot-word whose concealed pun supplies the hinge for double meaning. Then the first half ends with the word in one of its senses, while the second continues with the other. The following verse has been specially written by my friend Nansei to illustrate this. Since *matsu* in Japanese happens to mean both "pine" (tree) and "pine" (wait for in vain with longing), it has been possible to con-

struct an English version containing the same pivot-word:

> *Tasogare ya*
> *Matsukaze samushi*
> *Aki no yama.*

How mournfully the wind of autumn pines
Upon the mountainside, as day declines!

Here "pines" is an English kake-kotoba, acting as a verb with "the wind of autumn" and at the same time as a noun with "upon the mountainside," thus evoking a second but related image of "pines upon the mountainside." Sometimes the pun is partial, being made upon only one or two syllables of the Japanese word. It is just as though, in the example cited above, we were to take the compound "mountainside" and, with a play on its second element only, read it as containing the sound made by the unrequited wind, so that the "pines upon the mountain sighed."

Granting, then, that a transference of poetry, not to mention verbal play, must involve more of a commentary than a crib, it has sometimes been found necessary to amplify slightly in these paraphrases, incorporating either some of the implied impressions which every Japanese would at once supply from past experience of his social and natural environment, or some of the cognate material drawn from the commentators, both indigenous and English. Within the narrow compass of a haiku, this is perforce very little indeed. But what is known to any Japanese without inclusion in the poem may be the very thing that most needs to be explained to one who inevitably brings to the translation a widely divergent background of linguistic associations and cultural atmosphere.

The composition of haiku would indeed provide an invaluable discipline for overelaborate Western poets. A study of its extreme economy in words would prove most salutary to our poetry and show just how much unnecessary detail can be eliminated while still giving the season and setting by implication, even increasing the effect of actuality by making the reader draw the more upon his own memory and imagination. In creating as well as in translating a haiku, the subject, the time, and the place must be established in the reader's mind in the correct order if the total effect is to be clear and bright. But owing to the peculiar structure of Japanese thought and language, this is often the exact opposite to the presentation in English, and so the haiku must be translated backwards.

Most of the originals, though not all, are without titles, which have usually been retained where they exist and supplied where they do not. No doubt these will seem intolerably redundant and superfluous from the Oriental viewpoint; but an Occidental needs some assistance if he is to receive a poetic experience at all similar to that of a native. It is hoped that the heading added to each untitled haiku will either help to establish its mood or else drop some discrete hint as to its inner meaning, without being excessively explanatory. A title is perhaps preferable to a pedantic exegesis in prose, so disastrous to the poetry, and rather like trying to expound the point of a joke to someone without a sense of humour. A few notes on obscure allusions and uniquely Japanese references have had to be added, but these have been kept to a minimum. The translator is faced with two alternatives: either he can prefix a title and expand the text slightly with elucidatory matter; or he can append a description and discussion, as Miyamori, Blyth, and others do. But to the Zen outlook, this latter must seem quite irrelevant—clumsy, even though clarifying— and likely to deprive the reader in advance of the opportuni-

ty to make his own poetic discoveries. For the same reason, Buddhism avoids dogma and stresses method, so as not to prejudice realization. A rational explanation in words cannot then be substituted for real experience.

Although the poet may avail himself of the privileges of condensation and elaboration (and even of improvement, if that be possible) so abundantly justified by Edward Fitzgerald, whose masterly epitome of 'Attār's " Bird-Parliament" is the least literal and most poetic of all variations on an Oriental theme; nevertheless, a degree of amplification or alteration is only permissible if it captures or recreates the poetry of the original. And great care must be taken to avoid too liberal an accommodation to Western modes of life and categories of thought, which, as often as not, are diametrically opposed to Eastern ones, since until fairly recently such societies derived their cultural unity from Metaphysical Principles, lamentably lacking in ours, which can conceive of no social cohesion higher than the political and economic. A great many translations of Oriental scriptures have been made rather worse than useless by a failure to grasp this, as much as by the difficulties of attempting to transfer into our "tradesmen's languages," designed only for dealing with material things and external relations, those subtle and profound doctrines which have been expressed in multivalent languages much more suited to expounding the Traditional Metaphysic.

It may be laid down as a general rule of translation from Eastern languages that no word of specifically or exclusively European connotation should be used if some neutral alternative can be found. Proper names like "Sunday" or "January," or common nouns like "soul" or "narcissus" with their latent Christian or Graeco-Roman derivations and associations, should be eliminated with care from the translator's voluntarily limited vocabulary. To speak of "fine penmanship," as one of our foremost Orientalists has done with regard to a people who until last century used only the writing-brush, is both misleading and unnecessarily inept, since we already possess well-established and acceptable equivalents in such terms as "calligraphy" and "brushwork." The English vocabulary should be suitably restricted to select words which do not detract from, but rather help to conserve, the characteristic cultural ethos. That appropriate to a translation from the Arabic or Persian will obviously differ from one suited to rendering the Chinese or Japanese. It is here that the inherent taste of the poet, his intuitive sense of verbal congruity, is essential if the poetic flavour is to be preserved along with the overt meaning. But exotic idioms and expressions, as well as untranslatable Oriental words, should be employed very sparingly, else the style will break down into a semi-English jargon.

Although the haiku masters cultivate a deliberate nakedness and poverty of diction, allowing only a sparse indulgence in adjectives, adverbs, pronouns, and even verbs, and so making of this a poetry of nouns, postpositions (the Japanese equivalent of our prepositions), and interjections, to reproduce such a style in English would reduce the translation to a mere heading for a poem, rather than the poem itself. It would not even possess that "inverse poetry" which results from a plain bare statement such as can be found in Wordsworth; but would seem merely flat and stale, an effect of impoverishment rather than frugality, of the ordinary rather than the simple. Such dull conventionality is the deadly enemy of living poetry, and is to be avoided even at the expense of literal exactness.

The most famous of all haiku may be quoted again here to illustrate this need for stylistic and structural modifica-

tion, inevitable if something of the same *rensô,* or constella-
tion of ideas, is to be given in English. To present the reader
with a baldly literal version such as

Furu ike ya	The old pond!
Kawazu tobi-komu	A frog jumps in:
Mizu no oto.	The sound of the water!

is to fail completely to evoke in his mind's ear and eye the
associations and atmosphere which this verse has for every
Japanese, who can recite it by heart; and which have been
dissected and discussed at deadly length by both their critics
and ours. The poet must supplement this bare statement
with much that the Japanese memory and imagination offer
spontaneously, but which ours do not. He must give a
poetic realization, if he is to capture the atmosphere:

IN A TEMPLE GARDEN
The old green pond is silent; here the hop
Of a frog plumbs the evening stillness: plop!

Much of the effect of the original depends on the onomatopoeia, in which the assonance of short "o" sounds, repeated no less than five times, suggests to the ear the water-
sound when the frog jumps in. By a happy coincidence, it
has been found possible to reproduce these in the poetic
paraphrase.

Despite a few such liberties taken, a large proportion of
these versions in verse are quite literal, sometimes more so
than those previous renderings on whose foundations they
have in part been built. As an illustration of the method
adopted, a well-known haiku by Sôkan may be shown in
the various stages of its passage into English poetry:

Romanized Transliteration:
> Koe nakuba
> Sagi koso yuki no
> Hitotsurane.

Literal Pidgin-English Version:
> Voice if-were-not
> White-herons only snow's
> One-line-see?

Translation into Haiku-Form:

If they gave no cry,	5 syllables
See, those white herons would be	7 syllables
But one line of snow!	5 syllables.

Poetic Paraphrase into Couplet:

THE VOICE OF SNOW
That flight of egrets, if they gave no cry,
Would be a streak of snow across the sky

Few translations from Far Eastern languages make any attempt to find English parallels to the individual styles of Oriental poets. All tend to be turned into the same flat, tuneless, prosaic uniformity, so that Li Po and Tu Fu, to give a well-known example, whose styles are as diverse in the Chinese as, say, Shelley's and Wordsworth's, become almost indistinguishable in a translation devoid of rhythm and rhyme. Contrary to a current misconception, the Chinese poets wrote neither in Imagist free verse nor in Hopkinsesque "sprung rhythm." Some attempt has been made here, as above, to find equivalents not only for the varying subject-matter but also for the characteristic styles of the haiku poets, though unavoidably these must be coloured by the over-all style of the translator. But it is hoped that the reader will at least be able to distinguish

between Bashô, the wandering monk, unordained yet living by Zen, the most profound of haiku poets; Buson, the poet-painter, with his eye for the picturesque, his taste and sensibility; the bitterly unhappy Issa, filled with Buddhist compassion for all sentient beings; and Shiki, the Keats of haiku, a great master of poetic still-life who died young of consumption, and the first to feel the influence of English poetry toward the end of last century.

Obviously the basic principles of prosody must vary from language to language, since each manifests a different set of possibilities and limitations for the poet. Thus each language should conserve its own metrical forms and not seek to annex those of foreign tongues which it cannot assimilate. It is not necessarily, then, a question of attempting to reproduce in English the seventeen-syllable, three-line form of the haiku. As has been shown, this happens to be quite easy to do; but the result of being thus satisfied with a line-by-line rendering into prose almost invariably sounds devoid of time and tune. This is because the foundation of English verse is not a syllabic count, but a pattern of stress accents conflicting and collaborating with a pattern of quantities.

Recently, Kenneth Yasuda in his doctoral thesis *The Japanese Haiku* has made yet another attempt to import Japanese syllabic versification into English. But since the time of the Imagists, on whose work he bases his argument, the general trend of English poetry has been a steady reversion from the amorphous licence of their "free verse" to the older metrical forms. And the repeated failure to establish in English such classical measures as the hexameter, with its scansion by quantity alone, borrowed from Latin and Greek, which are much more akin to our own language in ancestry and structure than Japanese, should have been warning enough. One might as well attempt to write closed rhyming couplets with accentual metre in Japanese. His practice perforce belies his theory, since he cannot maintain the strict metronomic count of seventeen syllables, even with the aid of the most ungainly distortions of English word-order; his syllabic groupings are forced and arbitrary; inevitably he falls into the iambic and trochaic stressed rhythms which are as natural to English as equally unstressed alternations of five and seven syllables are to Japanese; and he has frequent recourse to rhyme. Nothing could demonstrate more clearly the need for the prosody of each language to respect its own boundaries.

Rather, the problem consists in discovering among existing English verse-forms a stanza which occupies a place corresponding to that of the haiku in Japanese versification, or one which might be adapted for this purpose. Although at first sight it might appear that nothing of any poetic value could be stated, let alone developed, in such a dwarfed poem, and that in consequence no equivalent is likely to be found, nevertheless the English literary tradition does happen to possess a comparably minute form. The smallest stanza of similar length capable of standing alone in English is the single rhymed couplet. Like the haiku, the couplet, with only eighteen to twenty syllables, is the most that can be comfortably spoken in a single breath, and so is best suited to short lyrical exclamations. It is often to be found in isolation as a complete poem, notably in the works of Robert Herrick, our most delicate miniaturist. Hitherto, its content has been epigrammatic, proverbial, obituary, or gnomic; but there is even a precedent in Herrick for its use as a nature poem; and Thomas Gray, as he wandered the fields near Blundeston with a friend, is said to have uttered the impromptu lines:

> Here pipes the wood-lark, and the song-thrush there
> Scatters his loose notes in the waste of air.

What critic, on the preconceived criterion of custom alone, would presume to decree that no new uses are to be found for old forms, banning technical discovery on the grounds that all has been exhausted in the past? Such academic prejudices merely preclude the opening up of fresh possibilities and so of any true originality, and invite the poet to disprove them by success in the expression of an unfamiliar content in the familiar form.

It is the couplet, therefore, which has been chosen for the paraphrases of haiku in this book. Lest it be objected that the haiku is in three lines and employs no rhyme, while the couplet has but two which do rhyme, it should be remarked that in chanting a haiku aloud twice, as is the Japanese custom, a pause is made after the kireji, which is usually placed at the end of the first line and announces the subject; then the second and third lines, which contain the counter-subject and their conjuncture, are read continuously as though one. Less often the caesura occurs after the second line, in which event the first and second lines are enjambed. Thus the effect to the ear is of a two-line, rather than a three-line, poem. But this threefold division of the theme will be found to be preserved inside the couplet form by means of punctuation and enjambement, thus giving it an effect of asymmetry. Without rhyme, moreover, the couplet would seem wanting to our ears in any sense of lyrical utterance, which the haiku most certainly has when recited by a Japanese. To clinch the meaning and music, we feel a need for rhyme, which would, on the other hand, sound intolerably strong in a language in which all syllables but one end in a vowel. These are the reasons why, contrary to the currently accepted practice of rendering rhymed and metrical poetry in the foreign tongue into unrhymed and unmetrical English prose, the very reverse will be found here.

As for the shortcomings of these verses, an apology can best be offered in the words of Lady Murasaki, from her *Tale of Genji,* Book 3, Chapter 6 (as translated by Arthur Waley):

> You may think that many of the poems which I here repeat are not worthy of the talented characters to whom they are attributed. I can only repeat that they were in every case composed upon the spur of the moment, and their makers were no better pleased with them than you are.

NOTES

1 (page 20). In his Third Series of *Essays in Zen Buddhism,* D.T. Suzuki relates an anecdote regarding the origin of this most famous of haiku. When Bashô was still studying Zen under his master, Butchô, the latter one day enquired concerning his progress in Buddhism. "After recent rain, the moss has grown greener than ever" was Bashô's reply. Butchô tested this with a further question: "What Buddhism is there prior to the greenness of moss?" and Bashô's second answer is said to have given rise to this verse.

2 (page 25). This was Bashô's witty solution to the problem of improvising a haiku on an impossible subject set by an admirer. Even to mention the names of the Eight Famous Views of Ômi would take several haiku. The remaining seven views are: the autumn moon seen from Ishiyama, the evening snow on Hirayama, the blaze of evening at Seta, the boats sailing back from Yabashi, a bright sky with a breeze at Awazu, night rain at Karasaki, and the wild geese alighting at Katata.

3 (page 29). Foxes and badgers are the notorious shape-shifters of Japanese legend, with the magic power of assuming human form at will to trick and mislead the unwary. Here the fox has changed himself into a prince to lure unfortunate court ladies into amorous adventure.

4 (page 43). The Japanese names for the morning-glory and the moon-flower are *asagao* ("morning-face") and *yûgao* ("evening-face").

5 (page 45). The most celebrated Zen garden in Japan, that of Ryôan-ji temple in Kyoto, dates from 1469 and consists solely of a courtyard of raked white sand in which are asymmetrically disposed fifteen stones, in groups of five, three, and two, at five places.

6 (page 56). Bashô's lord and patron, whose name Sengin means "cicada-song," died young.

7 (page 62). The *hototogisu,* or Japanese cuckoo, sings mostly at night and, unlike ours, has a threefold note—cuck-cuck-oo—

which it utters twice. It is believed to fly back and forth from this world to the "Farther Shore." As the bird of disappointed love, the inside of its mouth is red as though bloodstained by its anguished cry of longing, which is silenced only by absorption into Nirvāna.

8 (page 65). The lespedeza or bush-clover, called *hagi* in Japanese, is a graceful, fountain-like plant with showers of white or purple pea-flowers.

9 (page 66). Written on the death of the poet's child.

10 (page 69). *O-Bon* or *Bon Matsuri* is the Buddhist Festival of the Departed, celebrated from the thirteenth to the fifteenth of July, during which, in some regions, the ghosts of the ancestors are led back from the cemetery to their former homes by their descendants carrying paper lanterns. Being late summer, it is also the time for fireflies, on which the spirits of the dead are believed to ride.

11 (page 70). Bashô, on one of his poetic pilgrimages, fell in with a group of farmers holding a poetry-making party, at which the set subject was "The Full Moon." Failing to recognize the poet in his monk's disguise, the rustics asked Bashô to join them. When he began his haiku with the words "the new moon," they poured much good-humoured derision on the effort of the stupid monk. But after he had concluded his poem, they realized at once with delight and wonder that this could only be the work of the master haiku poet himself.

12 (page 76). When Kikaku presented his master, Bashô, with the preceding verse, the latter immediately countered with the remark "That is not haiku!" and composed this haiku, reversing uncompassionate destruction into the poetic gift of life.

13 (page 83). This haiku was sent to Bashô's friend and favourite disciple, Ransetsu. The *kiri* or paulownia tree is noted for dropping its leaves on the stillest of autumn days.

14 (page 97). A statue of Jizô, Patron Bodhisattva of children, who saves the wayfarer from wandering in the Six Paths of Existence, is often to be seen standing by a country roadside; for this reason he is here referred to as "the wet god."

15 (page 97). When asked on his death-bed for the customary

farewell haiku, Bashō replied that all his later poems had been last poems; but he offered this to his disciples as a self-portrait of the lifelong traveller who must again depart on the still uncompleted Way.

16 (page 101). Huge wooden statues of wrathful aspect, representing the two Ni-ô or Door Guardians, stand on either side of the gates of Buddhist temples.

17 (page 103). Should this species of stork, now almost extinct in Japan, fail to migrate before winter, it is unlikely to survive. To Kakei's screen-painting in words of the preceding haiku, his master, Bashô, has added this perfect finishing touch, thus turning the haiku into a tanka.

18 (page 104). Affixed to the sole of the Japanese clog or *geta* are two wooden cross-pieces, the imprint of which on the snow resembled the Sino-Japanese character for the number two.

19 (page 108). A marvellously compressed narrative. The father has been awakened at night by someone moving about in his room. He catches the thief and calls to his family and attendants to bring lights so that the thief may be identified—only to find, when they do so, that it is his own eldest son. But the father is the real culprit, since he has failed to inculcate strict principles of filial piety in his son. Said to have been composed by Sôkan during a renga contest in response to the couplet: "I wanted to kill him. I didn't want to kill him."

20 (page 109). In the Far East, the devotion of the mandarin duck and drake is taken as a symbol of marital fidelity.

21 (page 114). This haiku was found under the pillow of the poet's death-bed.

22 (page 114). The sacred mountain, which can be seen in whole or part throughout the year from some twenty-two provinces in Japan, is here coupled with the holiest day of the Japanese year. Although of Ainu derivation, the name Fuji may also be interpreted to mean "without equal" or "peerless," and hence is used as the metaphysical term for the Non-Dual.

BIBLIOGRAPHY

Blyth, R. H.: *Haiku* (4 vols.). Hokuseido, Tokyo, 1952.

——: *Senryû: Japanese Satirical Verses*. Hokuseido, Tokyo, 1949.

——: Zen in English Literature and Oriental Classics. Hokuseido, Tokyo, 1942 & 1956.

Chamberlain, Basil Hall: *Japanese Poetry* (chapter on "Bashô and the Japanese Epigram"). John Murray, London, 1880 & 1911.

Four Seasons, The: Japanese Haiku Written by Bashô, Buson, Issa, Shiki, and Many Others. Peter Pauper, New York, 1958.

Henderson, Harold G.: *The Bamboo Broom.* Houghton Mifflin, Boston, 1934.

——: *An Introduction to Haiku: An Anthology of Poems and Poets from Bashô to Shiki.* (A revised and enlarged edition of his *The Bamboo Broom.*) Doubleday Anchor Books, New York, 1958.

Japanese Haiku. Peter Pauper, New York, 1955

Keene, Donald. *Japanese Literature.* Wisdom of the East Series. John Murray, London, 1953; Tuttle, Tokyo, 1955.

Mackenzie, Lewis: *The Autumn Wind: Selections from the Poems of Issa, with an Introduction.* Wisdom of the East Series. John Murray, London, 1957.

Miyamori, Asatarô: *An Anthology of Haiku, Ancient and Modern.* (A revised edition of his *One Thousand Haiku, Ancient and Modern,* 1930.) Maruzen, Tokyo, 1932 & 1956.

Noguchi, Yone: *The Spirit of Japanese Poetry.* Wisdom of the East Series. John Murray, London, 1914.

Page, Curtis Hidden: *Japanese Poetry* (chapters on haiku). Houghton Mifflin, Boston & New York, 1923.

Porter, William N.: *A Year of Japanese Epigrams*. Oxford University Press, Oxford, 1911.

Yasuda, Kenneth: *The Japanese Haiku: Its Essential Nature, History, and Possibilities in English, with Selected Examples*. Tuttle, Rutland & Tokyo, 1957.

——: *A Pepper Pod*. Knopf, New York, 1947.

INDEX OF AUTHORS AND TITLES

Titles of haiku are shown in italics. Authors are entered under the names with which they signed the haiku included here, followed, when known, by their family names and dates but no attempt has been made to indicate other names an individual author may also have used. Titles of haiga and names of artists are not included as they will be found in the List of Illustrations at the front of the book.